COAST DOGS DON'T LIE

Jack Schofield

COAST

DOGS

DON'T LIE

*Tales from the
North Coast Sched*

SONO NIS PRESS
Winlaw, British Columbia

Copyright © 2009 by Jack Schofield

Library and Archives Canada Cataloguing in Publication

Schofield, Jack, 1927-
   Coast dogs don't lie : tales from BC's coastal airlines / Jack Schofield.

ISBN 978-1-55039-169-5

   1. Aeronautics--British Columbia--History.
2. Floatplanes--British Columbia--Pacific Coast--History.
3. Airlines--British Columbia--Pacific Coast--History.
I. Title.

TL523.S34 2009   629.13'09711   C2009-901579-X

Sono Nis Press most gratefully acknowledges the support for our publishing program provided by the Government of Canada through the Book Publishing Industry Development Program (BPIDP), The Canada Council for the Arts, and the British Columbia Arts Council.

Editing: John Eerkes-Medrano and Dawn Loewen
Cover design: Jim Brennan

Cover photo: Rich Hulina © 2003

Map: adapted from map created by Stuart Daniel, Starshell Maps (2003) for *Flights of a Coast Dog* (2nd ed.), originally published by Douglas & McIntyre

Photos: all from the collection of Jack Schofield, unless otherwise noted

Sketches: by Jack Schofield, unless otherwise noted

Some of the stories in this book were originally published in *Aviator* magazine or its earlier incarnations.

Published by
SONO NIS PRESS
Box 160
Winlaw, BC V0G 2J0
1-800-370-5228
books@sononis.com
www.sononis.com

Printed and bound in Canada by Friesens Printing.

Printed on acid-free paper that is forest friendly (100% post-consumer recycled paper) and has been processed chlorine free.

The Canada Council | Le Conseil des Arts
for the Arts | du Canada

To Colleen
Many great entries in our journey log

CONTENTS

FLYING UP THE COAST

Until 1980, British Columbia's coastal communities were served by several small seaplane airlines based out of Campbell River in the south, Port Hardy on the mid-coast and Prince Rupert in the north.

"Coastal communities" is a phrase that needs some clarification: most of the stops along the routes of the Beaver, Cessna and Otter seaplanes of these little airlines were Native villages, logging camps, private float camps and sport-fishing resorts. They were all classed as whistle-stops, and anyone wanting to book a seat or space for freight on the regular scheduled flight had to call in and reserve. None of these places had road access, and coastal packets and steamships had long given up trying to compete with the daily airplane service offered by the seaplane outfits. Since the people living and working in the myriad inlets, bays and coves along this mountainous coast's beautiful waterways depended on seaplanes for transportation and supplies, they hailed airplanes as city folk might call cabs.

The "North Coast Sched" was the name pilots hung on Gulf Air's daily flight out of Campbell River. It didn't go to the north coast, but only as far north as would permit its return before nightfall. Seaplanes don't fly at night, so the Otter or Beaver had to be back at base before the official grounding time as stipulated by Transport Canada. To call the service a schedule was also something of a stretch; it was rarely on time at any of the stops owing to a variety of delays from weather, passenger snafus and other unexpected events. As one wag put it, "We could be on time if we didn't have to deliver so many babies along the way." The "babies" were more often truck transmissions or other breakdown parts, or heavy grocery loads for the camps and cookhouses

Jack Gleadle, a pilot with Gulf Air in its early days, designed the company's thunderbird logo. It was painted green, as was the fleet: green was owner Don Braithwaite's favourite colour.

that dotted the charts of this area in those days.

Somebody sold a lot of white and orange paint in 1980, because that year all the aircraft of four of these coastal outfits, along with two Lower Mainland airlines, went through the paint shop of the newly minted upstart named AirBC. This new airline was about to change coastal aviation dramatically. The industry had seen such a change before, when Russ Baker created Pacific Western Airlines by amalgamating an assortment of B.C.'s coastal airlines. Now, as then, familiar names and faces were about to slip from the scene—as were places, when the criterion of economic viability was applied to the route structure of the newly created regional carrier. The big "A" now painted on the tail of almost every bush plane on the coast would make history of Gulf Air's long-familiar thunderbird logo, West Coast Air Services' "chicken hawk" emblem and Island Airlines' well-known orange triangle.

The pioneer operators who founded these services and who persevered and innovated through difficult years of attrition—the Michaud brothers of West Coast Air Services, Bob Langdon of Island Airlines, Don Braithwaite of Gulf Air and Gene Storey up in Rupert, to name a few—now slipped into history.

Each of these smaller-scale entrepreneurs walked into the sunset with a fat wallet, thanks to AirBC owner Jimmy Pattison, but they also took with them memories of an era of great adventure.

Some stories from that era are remembered here. Each chapter after the first begins with a "Walkaround"—the first thing a pilot does before getting into an airplane—to give an idea of what's coming up in the chapter. The stories are told in that inimitable form known in the trade as "hangar flying." Pilots usually serve up these stories with much zooming of the hands and great embellishment of the facts. The embellishment is provided here by the author, but readers must supply their own hand gestures as events of humorous, ordinary and sometimes tragic proportions are recalled—events that took place in a vanishing era of B.C.'s coastal flying history.

PACIFIC COASTAL AIRLINES

This map shows the area generally referred to as the mid-coast, which was served by Gulf Air from Campbell River and Port Hardy. Campbell River, Qualicum Beach and Nanaimo are off this map to the south (on the eastern coast of Vancouver Island). Rivers Inlet, Fitz Hugh Sound, Bella Bella, and Ocean Falls are off the map to the north of Vancouver Island.

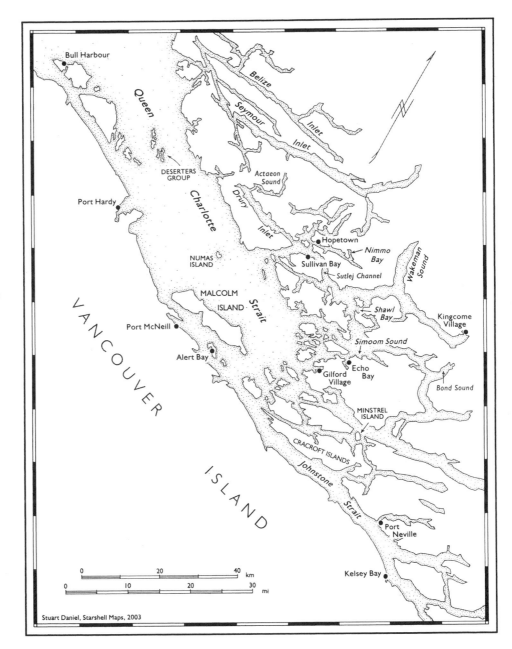

Stuart Daniel, Starshell Maps, 2003

Airline owners, pilots, dispatchers and engineers all share a common love of the craft.

12

1

THE DYNAMIC MUSEUM

Aircraft of the B.C. Coast

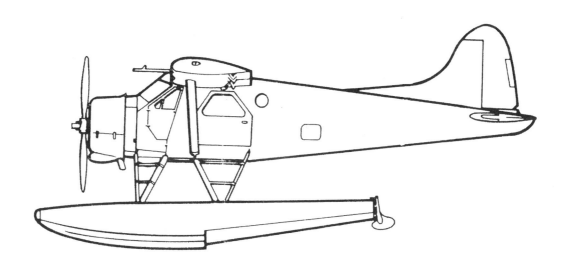

Designed in 1930 and powered by two radial engines designed in 1927, the Grumman Goose is still flying the coast of B.C., and it has to be one of the most durable aircraft ever built. Pacific Coastal Airlines operates four Goose from its base at Port Hardy, B.C.

An aircraft engineer friend of mine refers to the seaplanes flying along British Columbia's coast as the "dynamic museum." It's an appropriate name for airplanes whose engines have been out of production since the 1940s and which, even at that time, had been hurriedly built in large numbers from a design conceived—if you can believe it—in 1927.

The airframes in which these old engines are installed are themselves museum pieces, the oldest of which are the Grumman Goose from the 1930s, and the 62-year-old de Havilland Beaver and its 53-year-old stablemate, the Single Otter. That these are still the definitive bush planes flying the B.C. coast and, indeed, still in worldwide use, is understandable when you consider the dependability of both engine and airframe and the short take-off and landing (STOL) feature that continues to make them the very best planes for

Sometimes referred to as a "Spam Can" or a "Dollar Eighty-five," the Cessna 185 seaplane performs best with a maximum load of one skinny pilot, two loggers and two pairs of loggers' boots.

the job. Pilots love to fly them and have welcomed the many modifications made to keep these old birds flying during this era of great technological change. The Single Otter has been successfully upgraded by replacing the original 600-horsepower radial engine with the Pratt & Whitney PT6 turbine, but while there are a small number of turbine-powered Beavers in service, those are of a special design, and the stock Beaver continues its amazing career with the original engine—the R985 Pratt & Whitney nine-cylinder, 450-horsepower radial—beloved by

pilots worldwide for its inimitable sound and dependability.

On the other hand, the Cessna 180 and 185 seaplanes are sometimes referred to by their pilots as "Spam Cans"—a slight on the mass-production method of manufacture employed by Cessna in Wichita, Kansas. Despite this slur, the "Dollar Eighties and Dollar Eighty-fives" (the less derogatory nicknames) perform a useful service for the coastal airlines by handling the one- and two-passenger charters safely and economically. The 180 and 185 are the same airplane except for the

15

In 1946 B.C. Airlines operated a fleet of these little flying boats. The Seabee's versatility was its main appeal, despite being underpowered for commercial work.

engine; the 185 has more horsepower (300 versus 265) and is fuel injected. Cessnas are relatively fast for a seaplane (120 knots), as well as comfortable and forgiving—the latter quality referring to their inherent stability and pre-stall flight characteristics. They have what is referred to as a Johnson bar flap control—a manually operated lever providing instant flap when

the pilot selects it, an essential feature for seaplanes. Some years ago, Cessna decided to discontinue the manual flap control and provide an electric flap motor. This would have destroyed the aircraft's versatility, as electric flaps are slow to operate and would dictate different landing and take-off techniques. Island Airlines' president, Bob Langdon, flew down to Wichita to plead with the

16

COAST DOGS DON'T LIE

plane builder not to make that modi-
fication. He won the toss, and Cessna
continued to provide the bush-popular
Johnson bar and installed electric flaps
in the 206, which doesn't cut it as a
bush plane.

Cessnas seem to corrode faster than
other aircraft do from the effects of
salt water on their aluminum structure,
and they show metal fatigue in certain
places from the heavy pounding they
take from rough-water take-offs and
landings. These weaknesses result in
a high maintenance cost for operating them on the coast, but Cessnas
nevertheless do a great job and will

be around as long as there are coastal
seaplane operators.

Amphibious bush planes were a
great innovation because their ability to land on the runway as well as
on the water means that operators can
drop their passengers off at airports to
connect with ongoing airline flights.
"Amphibs" are, however, costly to
operate: they weigh more than straight
floatplanes, thus reducing the amphibs'
payload. Their maintenance cost is
also very high, because the mechanism
that retracts the wheel gear into the
pontoons requires special attention. In
addition, there are two kinds of amphib

Villi Douglas, long-term manager at Gulf Air's Port Hardy base, with two of the company's line pilots in 1981. Douglas was moved to Vancouver when AirBC took over the operation, but soon reappeared at his favourite place: "Colour me North Island" was his quip.

pilots: those who have and those who will, referring to the propensity to land with the gear in the wrong position. "I couldn't hear the tower's warning because the horn was making so much noise" might be the funny excuse, but the results of such pilot error are costly. Amphibians are equipped with mirrors out on the lift strut that allow the pilot to see the main wheels when they are extended. The nose gear located on the pointy end of each pontoon comes up and lies on top of the float deck when retracted, so the pilot can't miss seeing it. The gear is pumped up or down by a manual hydraulic pump, which becomes immovable once the gear is fully extended or retracted. This "hard handle" assures the pilot that the gear is locked in position.

At Port Hardy airport, when amphibs were in general use, then-base manager Villi Douglas instituted a procedure that required pilots to call base on their high-frequency (HF) radio as they were about to land at their destination. "Check you landing with the gear up," would be Villi's response; the pilot would have to acknowledge, "Gear up." Every so often, Villi would get paranoid when he sensed that a pilot might be taking things for granted and would insist on a double check. The records attest to the success of Villi's system.

Flying boats have always been

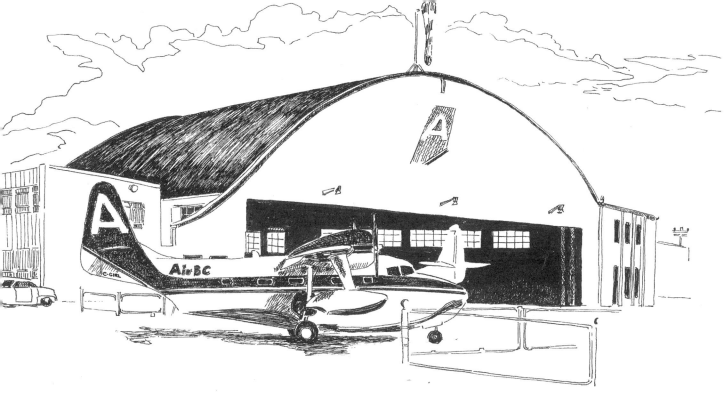

Following the Second World War, the Grumman company developed the definitive Mallard flying boat for corporate and feeder airline service. For 27 years, a fleet of these popular flying boats provided commuter service along the B.C. coast.

popular on the B.C. coast. In the early days of B.C. Airlines, following the Second World War, the Republic Seabee flying boat was the popular choice. "The Bee" was only a four-place airplane, was underpowered, had too short a wing and flew like a brick. But it did the job for several years before the Grumman Goose and Grumman Mallard, both amphibious boats, took over and performed yeoman service for B.C.'s coastal airlines. The Goose is still at work out of Port Hardy, where Pacific Coastal Airlines continues to operate the craft to serve the camps and communities in the local waterways.

It certainly lives up to the "dynamic museum" definition: it was designed in 1930 and is powered by two R985 radials—the same 1927-designed engine that powers the de Havilland Beaver. The Grumman Mallard, while much younger than the Goose, is no longer seen on the B.C. coast. As recently as 1979, West Coast Air Services operated six of these pretty flying boats, which came off the drawing board immediately following the Second World War. The Mallards plied the coast for 27 years, performing the job now done faster and more economically by commuter jets. AirBC retired the last two

Only 12 Huskies were built by Fairchild in 1947. Due to inadequate power, the aircraft lost out to de Havilland's Beaver in a U.S. Air Force bid. When re-powered with a 550-horsepower engine, the Husky became a great performer and was used for a short time along the B.C. coast.

Mallards, C-FGIRL and C-FGENT—dubbed "the Two Restrooms"—from coastal service in 1982.

The Fairchild Husky saw service with Island Airlines at Campbell River, with North Coast Air Services at Prince Rupert and for a short time with West Coast Air Services at Vancouver. The Husky was Fairchild's bid for the U.S. Army contract that was ultimately awarded to de Havilland's Beaver. It was an excellent design with many unique features, one of which was not the engine. The Husky was vastly underpowered, having an original 450-horsepower engine and becoming an outstanding performer only when it was re-engined with a British-built 550-horsepower radial. Fairchild Canada built only twelve of the craft, of which two museum pieces are the sole survivors.

Wheel planes are faster and cheaper to operate than seaplanes are, and logging camps or coastal communities that cleared runways in the bush could expect to be served by Twin Otter wheel planes or Britten-Norman Islanders, the latter being British-built airframes powered by American engines. Both types have STOL features, which permit big loads to be lifted from relatively short gravel runways. If you look closely at the Twin Otter, you

A great airplane for gravel strips, the Britten-Norman Islander is a 12-place light twin built on the Isle of Wight in the U.K. This airplane can land on a dime and give back 11 cents change. It is thought that the Canadian expression "Eh?" was born in this plane, because the props turn only inches from the pilot's ears. can see the Single Otter fuselage with a streamlined nose added and those wonderful PT6 turbines out on each wing. This great airplane is another de Havilland Canada achievement and has been put back in production by Viking Air of Victoria, B.C.

The Britten-Norman Islander deserves a tip of the hat for doing exactly what the pilot's handbook claims it can do. It is great to fly and displays a lot of British know-how, while at the same time embodying the Isle of Wight builder's seeming disdain for creature comforts in the plane's hard seats, lack of ventilation and inadequate cabin heater. Like the Twin Otter, the Islander is one of the few light twins that has what is jokingly referred to as a "welded" undercarriage—the wheels are always down and are designed to handle heavy landing shocks on the bush strips for which the plane is designed. Unlike the Twin Otter, however, the Islander cannot be mounted on floats.

21

The de Havilland Otter (top) and its partner, the Beaver, continue to operate as the definitive bush planes of the B.C. coast. The Single Otter has been successfully converted to turbine power and is used extensively in harbour-to-harbour flights between Vancouver, Victoria and Nanaimo.

KEN SWARTZ PHOTO

So long as there is a hinterland with limited alternative means of transportation, there will be a need for bush planes. Although some of these venerable aircraft lend themselves to modernization, very few fixed-wing aircraft are being built to replace them as they age. Helicopters might appear to be the answer to the problem, but most rotary-winged aircraft are powered by jet and turbine engines, which burn twice the fuel, at low altitude, that the old Beavers and Otters do. This is one of the reasons for the "fling-wing's"

high cost of operation. Also, helicopters are multi-taskers, and thus their ability to act as skyhooks defines their role more than does the transport of people.

The recent decision to put the Twin Otter back into production, and the large number of orders received from around the world for this 1960s aircraft, is evidence of the continuing demand for bush planes. The market is, however, too small to impel most plane builders to generate new designs. Watch for the "dynamic museum"—it will be flying in tomorrow's skies.

2

TALES FROM THE SCHED

Absolutely True Accounts of Bravery, Skill and Derring-do

Change Is Like a Second Chance

Alaska Pine, B.C. Forest Products, Canfor, Columbia Cellulose, MacMillan Bloedel, Powell River Company, Rayonier, Whonnock—the names of these giant forestry companies were common trade in the years following the Second World War. They were logging the coast as it had never been logged before. The world was rebuilding, lumber exports were at an all-time high and the logging companies were impatient with faithful but slow Union Steamships to deliver men and materials to their remote camps. Seaplanes could do in minutes what took a week for the coastal steamers, and aviation's entrepreneurs were quick to respond.

B.C. Airlines started with two airplanes in 1945 and exploded to become the biggest seaplane operation in the world, with bases in every key location along British Columbia's rugged coast. Queen Charlotte Airlines, the "accidental airline" of Jim Spilsbury, evolved from a radio repair operation to a full-instrument-flight, multi-engine regional air service. All this in a few short years—until the economy peaked and things began to level off. As the initial demand for products slowed and the province's economy stabilized, B.C. Airlines was sold off in pieces and a new generation of little guys emerged to serve the industries out of Vancouver, Nanaimo, Port Alberni, Campbell River and on up the coast to Port Hardy and Prince Rupert. Then, in the 1950s, Russ Baker came along, creating Pacific Western Airlines from a gaggle of little guys amalgamated with Queen Charlotte Airlines. More little guys surfaced to provide seaplane service to those customers who had been abandoned by the newly created large carrier, which now had its eyes on intercity routes and ultimately moved to Alberta.

It all happened again in 1980, when Jimmy Pattison acquired the routes and assets of another gaggle of "little guys"—AirWest, Gulf Air, Island Airlines, Pacific Coastal Airlines, Trans Provincial Airlines and West Coast Air Services—to create AirBC. Did another bunch of entrepreneurs go for the brass ring? Of course: Coval Air in Campbell River, five pilots in Gold River who called themselves Air Nootka, this writer's Orca Air in Alert Bay and Port McNeill, and

Waglisla Air, which offered service out of Vancouver to Bella Bella.

The history of B.C.'s coastal seaplane service is the story of little air services being amalgamated into big ones. The big guys inevitably move on to greater things, often leaving the float camp and lesser communities without service. In AirBC's case, the newly minted regional air carrier was soon sold off to Air Canada. The big "A" was painted over and replaced by the word "Jazz."

The stories related in this chapter took place, for the most part, before the birth of AirBC. In those early years, private float camps were numerous and many families lived in the bays and coves adjacent to big logging operations. There were also many "hand-loggers"—one-man logging shows—working on the coast. This larger and more varied clientele served by the early coastal airlines generated great stories—perhaps more so than does the current industry- and tourism-related airline trade.

If the past is a guide, one may expect a big guy to come along and inhale the whole thing once more. But fear not. History can't change one important phenomenon: where pilots gather, hangar flying will prevail.

High-frequency (HF) radio equipment, which was used in all aircraft on the North Coast Sched, provided dependable communication from base to planes. HF sends out a ground wave, which follows the earth's surface, whereas very high frequency (VHF) is a line-of-sight transmission. Though it was nothing like today's satellite radio, HF rarely failed—but there were times when pilots wished it would.

The Haul of Fame

Dispatch told the pilot, "You have six stops going up and two coming back—a piece of cake for an intrepid aviator like you." She smiled and passed him his flight sheet.

It was a glorious day, with just enough wind for a light chop on the water—good seaplane weather. He taxied the Single Otter out to the end of the spit, spinning the trim wheel along the way, judging the position of the trim to the weight for the six passengers and gear. Then he retracted the water rudders and firewalled the throttle (so to speak), checking first that the big hydromatic prop was in fine pitch and the fuel selector was pointing to the front tank. This ship carried enough gas to circumnavigate the globe, a nice feature for an airplane with a somewhat flexible flight plan. The Otter gathered speed. (Otters always "gather" speed—they seem reluctant at first, but once on the step, that funny stabilator on the tail and all that flap hanging down brings them into the air in an amazingly short run.) The other thing this pilot liked about the Otter was the sound—man, you knew you had something happening out there on the front end! That the decibel level in the cockpit exceeded the noise of your average sawmill was of little concern to this guy. Later, in his dotage, he would wear a hearing aid to compensate for the thrill; but, what the hell, "Give her when you've got her" was his motto today.

He slid her alongside the dock at Minstrel, his first stop. She came alongside standing off about four inches, dead slow and yawing into wind just as he had planned—almost as if he knew what he was doing. Had people been watching, they would have said, "Wow, that guy has done it before." But nobody was watching, so his expert, almost casual descent down the step rungs, scooping the aft painter and tying it off all in one fluid motion, was lost on everyone but himself. Jean Sherdal, the owner of the hotel at Minstrel Island, came down to the dock as he off-loaded the 20-odd 12-packs of Molson Canadian.

"When do you think the North Coast Sched will arrive on time?" Jean asked with a chuckle.

"When we're flying 737s on floats,"
the pilot replied. "And I don't have to wear blue jeans and workboots, and we have swampers aboard to do all the grunt work."

He undid the rope and pushed the float bow off the dock. The breeze did the rest as the big tail caught the wind and forced the nose around into it.

He dropped two loggers off at Port Elizabeth in Knight Inlet, then flew up the inlet to John Reid's lodge, where the two sport-fishing types got off and John put a passenger aboard destined for Campbell River.

"You'll be doing the tour with me for a while," he warned the new passenger, who had taken up the co-pilot seat beside him.

"Suits me," said the older man. "Great way to see the country."

The Otter bellowed up Knight to Tribune Channel, then into the Weldwood Camp in Thompson Sound, where two big loggers loaded a greasy truck transmission into the aisle. He instructed them to push it right up to the front, where he tied it down to the floor rings that de Havilland had thoughtfully placed in the corners of the cabin.

"You might like to move back a couple of seats," he suggested to the nice-looking, well-dressed woman who had seated herself up front when they had taken off out of Campbell. She thought it was a good idea, and stepped gingerly over the transmission to take a seat amidships.

He moved the groceries for Kingcome up behind the transmission to keep the aircraft in trim with the changing weight and balance, and then regained his seat as one of the loggers turned the Otter out from the dock. Before the engine caught, his co-pilot/ passenger remarked that the job of a pilot appeared to involve much more than just flying the plane.

"Yeah, we're sort of our own steve-dores on this route," he responded.

The next stop was at Kingcome Village, which meant climbing to about 1,200 feet in order to clear the pass out of Bond Sound into Kingcome Inlet. He then let down, carefully, so as not to cool the cylinders too quickly, and made a right-hand circuit of the Kingcome River, checking the fast river for logs and junk that could create a landing hazard. Small trees dropped into a river by a logging outfit some-times embedded themselves in the river bottom and could spear an aircraft during landing.

Docking at Kingcome was tricky. The river was fast, and the current coming out from under the dock tended to push the plane away from the dock. The pilot had to anticipate this effect by carrying enough power to offset the current. The ramp leading up to dry land presented an obstacle for the dockside wing, and the turn-in had to be timed just right. Also, the logging company had its own Beaver floatplane, which would be tied up at the end of the rather short dock, requiring the pilot to come alongside behind the Beaver and miss the ramp by one foot at the wingtip. He'd have to carry enough power to offset the current but not enough to crunch the Beaver's tail. If he didn't do it right, he'd be in deep doo-doo. Nobody saw him carry this off with aplomb either, but there you go—life on the North Coast Sched wasn't Hollywood.

Dave Dawson Jr. met the plane. He was a cheerful guy with a wry sense of humour and was there to pick up one of the passengers who had boarded back in Campbell River. Dave would take the passenger upriver to the village in the outboard-powered dugout canoe; he had brought two passengers down from the village who were now boarding the plane. Dave knew all of the pilots. He called out as he hauled the tail skeg around and over the dock, "I'm sur-prised they still let you fly this thing."

"Only on good days," the pilot yelled back. The big plane silently swung around and, carried by the 15-knot current, headed downriver. The 84-inch prop cranked over and then

During the logging and construction boom of the 1950s, Sullivan Bay was the acknowledged pit stop for itinerant seaplanes. Today it is a popular destination for pleasure craft. Many of the regular patrons of Sullivan Bay have built floating summer homes at the back of the bay. One of these houses sports a private helipad.

28

blurred as the R1340 Pratt belched blue smoke, its bark reverberating off the camp cookhouse as the pilot laid the power to it and lifted off the river.

This was usually the last inbound stop, but today he had to fly up Sutlej Channel to Sullivan Bay, where the pretty lady would get off to join a boater friend. As he levelled off at 100 feet, tracking the shoreline of Kingcome Inlet, the HF radio stopped hissing in his David Clarks and Noreen's voice came across the ether: "Check you off King-come for Sullivan." Then she added,

"We have a pick-up for you at Warner Bay—one passenger for Campbell."

"Check one out of Warner for Campbell—roger." Warner Bay was about a 20-minute flight from Sullivan. The pilot checked his watch, estimating that he would still be in good shape for grounding time on this fine day.

"I thought you were too old to fly airplanes." Pat Finnerty, the owner of the camp, grinned at the pilot on the Sullivan Bay dock as the pretty lady carefully descended the slippery step rungs. It was the pilot's task to hold her

One of the frequent stops on the daily sched route was Sullivan Bay, the most popular watering hole on the mid-coast since 1945. This sketch was made by Ed Price, father and father-in-law respectively of owners Lynn Whitehead and Pat Finnerty. Ed was responsible for all the unique signage on the docks.

ED PRICE DRAWING

hand and guide her down. Then he went back into the plane and tossed her bag to Finnerty, who, distracted by her beauty, nearly dropped the bag.

"Need gas?"

"No, I'm in good shape," the pilot replied while looping the rope around the foot rung on the float strut. "I could handle a cup of your gut-wrenching coffee, but I don't have time—the Dutchman at Warner is going to town."

"Life's a bitch." Finnerty waved, then turned to the young beauty, whom he escorted down the dock.

Warner Bay is a big open bay off Seymour Inlet and very close to Tremble Island, which lives up to its name when the tiderip roars through that narrow entranceway. Airplanes don't have to wait for slack tide, so the pilot landed in Warner Bay and proceeded up a narrow channel—river-like, but a saltwater river, so narrow that the Otter's 58-foot wingspan brushed the branches of the willows and alders overhanging the waterway on both sides. He had flown into the bay following a slightly inland route so that he could check the inside lagoon to be sure that no other aircraft were coming out of that narrow channel—there was no room to pass. He docked the Otter alongside the passenger's house, and the man boarded while still doing up his shirt and tying his tie, readying himself for the big city.

"Check you off Warner inbound." It wasn't Noreen this time—the pilot guessed she had gone home at shift change. "We have another three for you—one at Actaeon Sound and the other two at East Cracroft." He had by this time identified the voice as Val's and replied that he would be landing in Actaeon in five because it was so close. He could get to Boat Harbour on East Cracroft by about 17:35. She advised that there were two to pick up there, and would he think it possible to go back into Minstrel and pick up a 75-horse Merc urgently required for repair in Campbell?

"Yeah, sure—Actaeon, then Cracroft, then Minstrel for an outboard to Campbell."

He checked his watch and figured he was still okay for time—gas was no problem.

Landing at Actaeon required some local knowledge of the rocks in the landing area adjacent to the camp. At flood tide the water ran white around these rocks, and at least one plane, to

his knowledge, had come to grief landing here. So he was particularly careful and carried it off without a hitch. There was no sign of anyone on the dock, but a backpack had been placed to indicate that the passenger wasn't far away. This meant there was time to double up to the cookhouse. The cook at Actaeon was known for his pastries, and there were lots of goodies left over from the day's meals.

"Take a bag full of assorted." The cook laughed while passing him the bulging bag. The pilot poured a Styrofoam cup full of black battery-acid coffee, thanked the cook and headed back to the plane. His new passenger was aboard and soon joined the others in catcalls for the pilot to share the booty. He first selected a large lemon-curd Danish, resplendently sugar-iced, before passing the bag back to his laughing passengers. After take-off he wiped the throttle lever clean of the sugar icing and set course for East Cracroft.

The passengers to be picked up at Boat Harbour on Cracroft Island were two hippies who had been living on the island in a tent. There was no dock for the plane, so the pilot just shut down the engine and drifted around in the shallow water about 60 feet offshore. The two passengers waded out to the plane and boarded barefoot and

"A couple of guys with their gear," was how these sport fishermen booked their seats on the North Coast Sched. The author (right), with amphibious Single Otter UJM at Shawl Bay, around 1987.

dripping. Another passenger passed them the bag of pastries, and one of the hippies quipped: "What, no in-flight movie?" He received the stock pilot response: "Yeah, we flash your life before your eyes."

At Minstrel, the Mercury outboard was on the dock but nobody was around to help with the loading and to explain where it was going. A guy in a boat yelled that he would be right there. "Right there" turned out to be eight minutes, and the pilot started to get anxious about the time. The motor

was awkward in the aisle, and a couple of passengers had to move their seats. He knocked two seats down and folded them up to the wall to get the motor in place.

"Off Minstrel inbound," he called on the HF radio.

"You're going to hate me," she responded. There's an urgent breakdown part at Apple River up Loughborough."

"Jeez, that's a long haul from here. What's grounding time, again?"

"Stand by." The HF went into hissing mode for about a minute.

For obvious reasons, seaplanes aren't permitted to fly at night, but this is not to say it has never happened. "Finding the water," as he would with a glassy water landing, this pilot would pray that his landing path was free of logs, small boats and other unseen obstacles such as Transport Canada inspectors.

32

"Nineteen twenty-two."

He thought for a moment, then re-plied, "Okay, will do—Apple River next."

The hissing stopped again. And ..."

"Oh, no!"

"Right on your way home—Blind Channel at the restaurant—two for Campbell. We're ordering a Distinguished Flying Cross."

"Make it an Extinguished Flying Cross—I'm sacked!"

"You will be held in high regard by management."

"I'm not impressed."

More hissing in the earphones.

He landed at the Campbell River Spit four minutes before grounding time. As he taxied up the river toward the dock, he saw two women standing on the end of the dock with a big sign. It said, "Welcome home—All records broken—13 stops." The two dispatch-ers were laughing and waving.

His pants stuck to the leather seat cushion as he stepped out and, using the lift strut for support, slipped down to the dock. This time, someone finally noticed his expertise as he scooped up the rope and made fast all in one fluid motion.

"Hey, you've been practising," the dock boy chirped.

ART COX

I know of a pilot who flew a horse in the back seat of a Piper Super Cub. It was a small horse, but so is the Super Cub. The beast somehow got its legs untied, kicked a hole through the side of the fabric-covered fuselage and bent a few structural members, forcing the pilot to land earlier than anticipated. Dogs figure larger than horses in most pilots' experience, and this account wears the blue ribbon as best in show.

A Dog Day Afternoon

Jack Gleadle was flying for Trans Mountain Air out of the Campbell River Spit. He took off one morning with no passengers aboard and only two mail sacks for freight. The first mail sack was for Port Neville, up Johnstone Strait at the mouth of Port Neville Inlet—a flight of about 12 minutes from take-off. Since the inlet was whitecapping from a strong outflow, Jack decided to land straight into wind and lay up alongside the dock on what is generally referred to as the co-pilot's side of the airplane. As usual, the postmaster and his dog were waiting for Jack on the dock. The postmaster held the lift strut as Jack came ashore, leaving his mail and picking up the outgoing mail sack. Jack gave the friendly sheltie a pat on the head as he quickly boarded the Otter and, with a wave to the postmaster, poured the coal to the R1340 and took off up the inlet.

Greenway Sound, a popular boaters' destination on the north side of Broughton Island, had an ice cream machine, a popular attraction. Greenway became a favoured stop for the sched flight.

The Otter was airborne almost immediately in the strong outflow, and Jack executed a cautious 180-degree turn downwind to his next destination at East Cracroft Island, a summer fishing resort about 15 miles up the coast. Landing there after the short flight, he found the dock jammed with pleasure boats, so he just shut down close to the dock and waited for his passengers to come out in a boat. As the little boat approached the plane, everyone in the craft started pointing and yelling. Jack couldn't figure out what they were yelling about until he opened the door. There, on the deck of the offside pontoon, was the little sheltie from Port Neville.

Needless to say, the dog enjoyed the ride home in the cabin of the Otter better than it had the hair-raising trip on the pontoon. The postmaster was pleased and totally amazed that his canine buddy had survived the trip. He told Jack that when he saw the dog jump onto the float as the plane left the dock, he had leapt into his boat and followed the plane, expecting the dog to fall off into the water. Everyone was astonished that the dog had survived the trip by lying down flat on the float deck in the low-pressure zone atop the pontoon.

Jack Gleadle got home that night at about nine. Two phone messages were waiting for him, one from *Paris Match* and the other from a Hong Kong newspaper, each wanting to get the story about the amazing dog that flew the North Coast Sched.

Postscript: Several years later, when I was the one flying that scheduled flight, I asked the postmaster at Port Neville about the story. He confirmed that it had happened and that now the dog wouldn't come down to the dock when a seaplane arrived. Nor would the anxious canine allow anyone to take his picture. It seems the story had got around, and the dog had become quite a celebrity. Now, whenever boaters armed with cameras stopped at the dock, the sheltie would hightail it for home. He'd had enough of the paparazzi.

I have flown a grizzly bear in a Single Otter seaplane. The bear was locked up in a cylindrical cage just a few feet behind my seat. He was able to extend his claws far enough through the cage's wire grille to rip the leather on my seatback. Startled by the movement of the seat, I turned and looked into eyes that said "Kill." That was a chilling experience, but chilling is not the word I would use to describe my next airborne encounter with animals.

Bringing Home the Bacon

It was a very hot day in July. All the seats except the pilot's had been removed from the Beaver, and the entire cabin was lined with a heavy plastic drop sheet. The three women in the office were smirking when he walked in to pick up his flight sheet. When he read the sheet he became puzzled.

"One stop? How come only one stop?"

The three women giggled in unison.

"You have five VIPs," chuckled Val, the duty dispatcher. The other two women couldn't contain themselves. "VIPs," they chorused, bursting into laughter.

"To Fanny Bay." This was Doreen, the acting base manager, who was normally something of a sobersides but who was now laughing uncontrollably. She was looking down at the flight line at the fleet tied to the dock.

Dock boys are a pilot's best friends when loading or docking the aircraft. They were commonly referred to as "ramp rats" when servicing wheeled or amphibious aircraft on the ground, but as "dock swine" when working with seaplanes. Pictured here are three popular dock swine at Gulf Air's Campbell River seaplane base, around 1980.

"They have boarded your passengers—they're waiting for you." Big grin.

"Don't ham it up," Paula gasped, before she exploded with laughter.

The pilot, grinning now but not certain why, craned forward to see what was going on down on the dock. Just two dock boys waiting for him. Two dock boys—strange. With some misgivings, and knowing he was being had, he waved goodbye to the women and headed down to the dock. The Beaver was on the very end of the dock, facing toward the mouth of the river and pointing in the opposite direction from the other planes. He smelled something foul. It got stronger as he approached the Beaver. His grin

faded to a smile and then a poker face as he reached the plane and heard his passengers. He looked inside just as the loudspeaker came on. Valerie's voice intoned, "Five VIPs to Fanny Bay." Then laughter echoed over the speaker: "Very Important Pigs!"

There were five pigs in the Beaver, each immobilized by being tied into a gunnysack with only its head showing. They were very unhappy pigs. Unhappy pigs squeal a lot and urinate a lot and defecate a lot, and gunnysacks leak like a sieve.

"Jeez!" said the pilot, but he had little time to pause, because the dock boys, wearing big grins, had untied the plane and were turning it out into

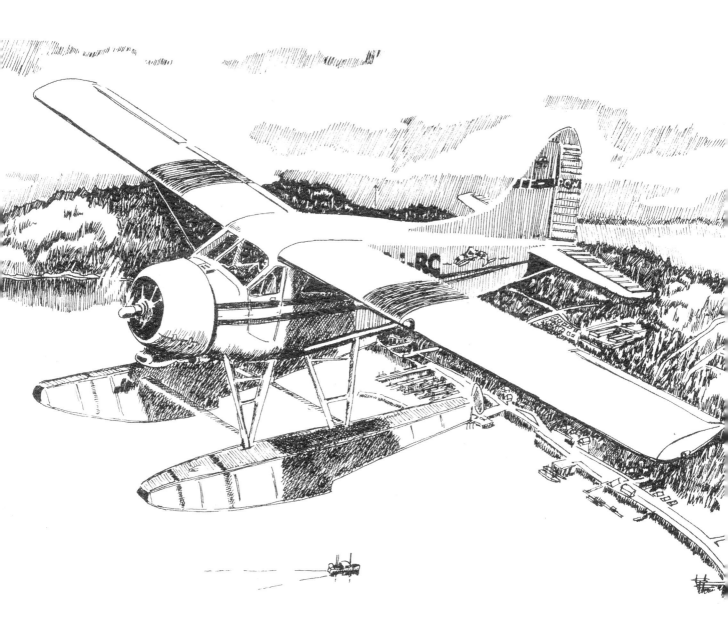

the river. He jumped onto the nearside pontoon and scrambled across the co-pilot area, now devoid of its seat, to the left-hand pilot seat. The passenger door slammed behind him, and the heat in the plane, combined with the foulest smell imaginable, hit him like a hammer.

The aircraft was now caught up in the river current and was showing a mind of its own. He pumped the throttle five times, snapped on the master switch and hit the starter switch after only two blades—to hell with the engineers and their preferred starting procedure. He snapped on the mags, and the R985 came through as usual.

He opened the pilot-side door and held it open with his foot, despite the sudden blast of prop wash. He was holding his breath while undoing the tension on the window knob. The Plexiglas slid down into the door with a thump, and the door banged shut. He stuffed his head out the window into the slipstream and dared to breathe—the sweet smell of engine exhaust. The pigs, rolling in their own excrement, screamed in panic. Ahead, through the windshield, he spied the end of the spit and a view of open water with a no-wind condition. Water rudders up fast, prop full fine, throttle up to 36 inches, 20 degrees of flap as she came up on the step and airborne—all without

breathing. Head as far out the window as possible, and into a 100-knot wind.

Call up those lovely women.

"Campbell River—JBP." He couldn't think of anything clever to say. "How come I won the toss?"

"You're such a nice, agreeable man, Jack."

"You owe me," he said.

"We're all married women and true," they laughed.

They went silent as other planes in the fleet, growing tired of trying to get a word in edgewise, broke in on the transmission. He put his head back out the window and proceeded up Phillips Arm to land in Fanny Bay.

A man met the plane, removed the squealing pigs and the plastic drop sheet, washed the sheet in the water and rolled it up. Then he walked off, waving goodbye to the pilot as if everybody were a pig farmer. The pilot got back in the plane and flew home.

Back at the office, they gave him a full day's pay and the same mileage as the highest-time pilot for the day. Then they told him to go home. He went back to his little apartment and took a bath.

Much later in life, this pilot lost his senses of smell and taste. The doctors said his condition was caused by a virus, but he believes it was a delayed reaction to those five VIPs.

There were 52 whistle-stops along the route of Gulf Air's North Coast scheduled flight. Each day a number of the route's logging camps, Native villages or float camp communities would phone in to book a pick-up or to advise that freight would be dropped off at the airline office for delivery on the sched—"A lot of perishables in the groceries, so don't forget them" would be a common admonishment. Unpredictable things were always happening along the way to delay flights. This one tops them all.

Mystery Flight

The day had dawned clear to the blue, with a light breeze creating no more than a ripple on the surface of Kingcome Inlet. Martha had awakened early and was preparing herself for the trip from her little village to Campbell River for a doctor's appointment. The seaplane that would carry her would land in the Kingcome River at about noon to pick her up. She would need all the time available to get her grandchildren ready for school, pack her things for the overnight stay and make her way downriver to meet the plane. Out on the river bank, in front of the village, Dan Willie Jr. and his father, Dan Sr., were preparing their 25-foot aluminum herring skiff for a trip to nearby Echo Bay, where they would purchase the family groceries for the next week. Echo Bay was about a 45-minute trip in the skiff, and they were looking forward to the outing—maybe they'd do a little fishing along the way.

Minstrel Island was an important stop for coastal steamers from the early 1900s until 1945, when seaplanes took over. The island was so named because early residents would perform a minstrel show for visiting ships. The hotel was built in 1904 and was still operating when this writer flew there in the 1970s and 1980s. A succession of owners "improved" the island by tearing down this historic building.

40

Down in Campbell River, the Single Otter C-GLCP had taken off from the spit with eight passengers, two mailbags and several cartons of groceries, which were stacked in the aisle. Harold, the Otter pilot, was congratulating himself for getting away exactly on time—08:00 on the nose—but he knew he would need a lot of good luck to keep the North Coast Sched on time at each of the six stops ahead. His first stop would be at Port Neville to drop one of the mailbags. Then he would continue down that inlet to the logging camp, where two of his passengers would get off. Harold checked his dispatch sheet and noted that there were no pick-ups until he got to Minstrel Island, the fourth stop on his flight. He loved flying the Otter, but it was slow to manoeuvre on the water, and the 58-foot wingspan was sometimes

a disadvantage when there were many fishing boats on the docks at his destinations. At 08:17 he began the letdown into Port Neville Inlet.

Meanwhile, at Kingcome Village, Martha had seen her grandkids off to the village school and had put her suitcase on the bed ready to be packed. Out on the river, Dan Jr. and his dad had launched the skiff and were halfway downriver toward the seaplane dock at the logging camp. The 75 on the stern was more than a match for the swift, 15-knot current as they approached the mouth of the Kingcome River, where its brown silt discoloured the deep turquoise of the inlet.

Harold was already behind schedule as he flared LCP onto the water at Minstrel Island. He hoped his pick-up passengers were there at the dock and ready to jump on. Ah, good! Two people were standing there waiting for him. Also, a stack of boxes—there was nothing on the dispatch sheet about those, but surprises like this were common on the sched.

He laid the Otter alongside the dock and slipped, effortlessly, to the float deck, scooped the rear strut rope and made it fast to the dock cleat. Clicking noises came from the Pratt & Whitney as it started to cool down.

"These are my wife's good dishes—she would like you to be very careful," said the elderly man as he attempted to lift one of the cartons.

"Let me," said Harold, swiftly loading the four boxes through the big double door into the aft cargo compartment.

As Harold was taking off from Minstrel and banking around the corner on his way up to the head of Knight Inlet, Martha, the passenger he would pick up later at Kingcome, was snapping her suitcase closed. She had phoned around to arrange for the ride downriver, and Thompson Leggat had agreed to meet her at the riverbank—he would run her down in the outboard-powered dugout canoe.

On the herring skiff, now in Sutlej Channel, Dan Willie Jr. was suggesting to his dad that they cut the speed back and troll for a salmon—it would be nice to catch a coho or a spring for dinner. They could do the shopping at the Echo Bay store and still be home by one o'clock.

Harold landed the Otter in the dammed-up river at the head of Knight Inlet. It was a nice place to land, being a man-made water runway. There was no wind, so Harold had landed straight in and was taxiing the dogleg up to the seaplane dock. He dropped two passengers and picked up one plus a generator motor, which was lashed down right at the step up to the cockpit compartment. He taxied down to the bend in the river and took off in the direction opposite to his landing, clearing the log dam by at least 50 feet. His next stop would be near the mouth of Knight, at John Reid's lodge; then he would fly through the pass on Gilford Island into Simoom Sound. He would pass up the stop at Echo Bay, where Bill and Nancy were to be picked up. He would do Wakeman Sound first, then Kingcome, and stop at Echo on the way back. He was behind schedule by about 25 minutes—not bad, he thought.

Martha heard the Otter circling overhead, checking out the swift Kingcome River for logs and other debris before it landed. As Thompson laid the dugout canoe onto the logging company's dock, the Otter came into view just falling off the step. "Perfect timing, Martha," he exclaimed. "There she is!"

The Otter discharged its last inbound passengers to the logging operation and Martha mounted the step. Everybody aboard was now outbound, and Harold had only the two at Echo Bay and three at Port Elizabeth to pick up before heading down Johnstone Strait for home.

As the aircraft droned along on its journey down Kingcome Inlet, Harold busied himself with the journey logbook, filling in the times aloft for each of the legs he had travelled. In the cabin, Martha peered out the window at the familiar waters of Kingcome Inlet 200 feet below. Suddenly, there appeared an alarming sight—an aluminum boat upside down in the water, and two men seemingly floating on the water with their arms outstretched. Martha didn't know that she could have slipped off her seat belt and walked up the aisle to alert the pilot. Instead, she called out to him—but from her seat at the back of the plane, no one heard her call against the roar of the 1340. She fretted but remained in her seat.

When they landed at Echo Bay, she grabbed the pilot's arm as he made his way down the aisle and told him what she had seen. Harold didn't waste time. Leaving Bill and Nancy on the dock, he took off out of Echo Bay, retracing his flight up the inlet. There, ahead of him, something was in the water just as the passenger had claimed. He descended to about 50 feet and banked steeply. It was a boat—one of those aluminum herring skiffs—upside down. He came around 180 degrees, pumped on flap and throttled back for the landing. The Otter touched down and drifted to a stop right by the half-submerged hull. Not a sign of anyone in the water.

"Are you certain there were people in the water? Yes? Well, there's no one here now. I'll take off and search the area, and I'll call the base to alert the Mounties' marine detachment."

The pilot of the North Coast Sched did just that and found no trace of the people reported to be in the water near the boat. Another small boat in the vicinity had arrived back at Kingcome about that time. Questioned later, those villagers said they had seen nothing on their way up the inlet. It was confirmed much later that the overturned boat was Dan Willie's. He and his son were never given up by Kingcome Inlet, and no one ever came up with an explanation of how the two experienced boaters had perished in the waters of the inlet on such a calm day.

The Single Otter was late getting to Campbell River that day. Several of the passengers who had waited to be picked up complained that they had been inconvenienced. Couldn't the airline do a little better in the future?

Once, when I was moving a logger and his family and all their worldly goods from one camp to another, the family dog threw up on my hand and all down the power quadrant—this during take-off. On another occasion, while flying on a turbulent day, I reached back to seize the journey logbook from the pocket on the back of the pilot seat and found the book missing. I stuffed my hand deeper into the pocket, and it came out dripping. Seems a considerate passenger had carefully removed the book, placed it on the floor and then vomited into the pocket. Another pilot recalled that while flying with the door off, for a group of parajumpers, one of the jumpers had puked out the door. The slipstream blew it all back into the cockpit, completely covering the pilot's sunglasses and obscuring his view. One other incident—nauseating, but thankfully without the vomiting—bears telling before getting back to the true romance of flight.

Every Man to His Trade

QRI was a Single Otter amphibian powered, in those days, with the 600-horsepower Pratt & Whitney R1340. It stood near the fuel bay at Port Hardy airport awaiting two passengers and what was described in the flight manifest as a full load of "household effects." The destination was Taleomey, in South Bentinck Arm, near Bella Coola. It was a very hot day and all the doors of the plane had been propped open, but the big cabin was stifling from the intense sunshine beating down on it. The concrete tarmac was radiating visible heat from the afternoon sun when the two (in fact, three) passengers, a man and a woman with an infant, arrived in a dilapidated stake truck loaded to the gunwales. The two adults were tree planters heading into camp for the season. They were travelling with their own personal tent city to set up in the bush. Nothing was packed—everything was loose, from

The flight panel of the Single Otter as it was originally designed, when it was powered by the Pratt & Whitney R1340 radial engine.

44

tents to toothbrushes, and each piece had to be loaded aboard the plane separately.

An amphibious Otter stands very tall—a three-step float ladder gets you to the float deck, and then it takes three more rungs of the boarding ladder to reach the cabin. I must have made 100 trips up and down the ladders in that heat to get the passenger cabin fully loaded. There was no "ramp rat" on duty to help, because it was a Sunday. The young woman laid a blanket out on the tarmac at the foot of the ladder and proceeded to change the infant's diaper. She used cloth diapers and saved them—complete with contents—stuffing the fragrant missile into a carryall that already contained three or four used ones from the road trip. This too went aboard.

All the seats in the Otter had been folded up against the fuselage to make room for the load. The exception was the seat on the starboard side, up front at the flight deck bulkhead. The young hippie-like mother, clutching her baby, climbed in through the pilot's door and took this seat, while her man sat beside me in the co-pilot seat. He had a singular appearance, having made his own sunglasses from heavy copper wire containing blue bottle-glass lenses. They were like John Lennon's glasses, very small, and the blue glass hid his eyes completely and cast a coloured shadow on his face.

The Otter was jammed full to the roof with aromatic cargo as we taxied out to the numbers on runway 07. The air in the cabin was foul. The combination of dirty diapers with the couple's "eau de tree farm," plus the mildewed tents and gear, drove me to stick my head out the pilot-side window both while taxiing and immediately after take-off—all reminiscent of an earlier flight with a different species aboard.

When I had off-loaded all that stuff at the destination, I was absolutely sacked. An onlooker who helped turn me out from the dock called out to me before I closed the pilot's door: "Every man to his trade!"

ART COX

In the days before the ban on smoking in public places, the coastal airlines allowed cigarette smoking during flights. Drinking, though, was not allowed, and most pilots would not let someone who was obviously drunk get on board, because this posed a safety hazard. Detecting someone under the influence of marijuana or other "soft drugs," however, was not so easy to do.

Take This Man's Name: A Near Chainsaw Massacre

The pilot's name was Rob. He was very handsome—perhaps debonair was the right word. He came from wealth and a good family from the right side of the tracks. The lady dispatchers loved him and always gave him the good flights. The last I saw of him, he was flying the "heavy iron" for AirBC out of YVR (Vancouver) to YYJ (Victoria), and he would appear in the waiting room looking resplendent in the blue serge AirBC uniform. AirBC was taken over by Air Canada, so I guess Rob will now be looking good up in the front end of something big with a maple leaf on it, and his flight bag will have all kinds of stickers telling us lesser beings where he has been. Rob deserves that; he could carry off the true derring-do pilot image even when flying a Single Otter with a bunch of drunken loggers in the back. He was the guy, at Gulf Air in Campbell River, who coined the term "tankers" to describe, derogatorily, those pilots who always carried enough gas to get home and have the required 45 minutes' reserve left in their tanks. Rob would come back on what could best be described as a whiff in the aft tank for reserve, and he would be pleased about it. Truth is, he was really good at the business of coastal flying.

We were sitting around in the pilots' ready room this day. I must describe the room, because Gulf Air's ready room was the ready room from hell. Tired old furniture from somebody's basement, government-green paint job, airplane pictures stapled to the wall and as many *Playboy* centrefolds as possible sticky-taped on top of the Transport Canada NOTAMs. (A NOTAM is a notice to airmen, usually advising pilots of some unimportant thing like rockets being fired by the military in some particular place at a particular time; Pamela Anderson's boobs were obviously more important than being shot down by friendly fire.)

Anyway, all of us except Rob were sitting there ("all" would be about five pilots) waiting to hear our names called out on the loudspeaker by the dispatcher. "Chuck, you've got FHT on the local sched. Pick up your dispatch sheet and get going. Your passengers are loaded"—that sort of thing. On this particular day, some of Rob's

passengers were just that—loaded. He was flying the Single Otter XUY on the North Coast Sched. He had taken off at about eight o'clock that morning, stopping at seven different spots along the coast, dropping off people and freight and picking up people and freight. His last stop was at Fanny Bay in Phillips Arm, where he picked up four loggers from the local logging show. One of them, a faller, was carrying his chainsaw, which Rob had stashed under one of the passenger seats. This logger was seated in the farthest aft seat on the starboard side, opposite the big freight doors on the port side. There were 11 seats in the Single Otter, and Rob now had a full load.

Fanny Bay is about 15 minutes' flying time from Gulf Air's base at Campbell River, and Rob called off Fanny Bay estimating Campbell in 15. He did this on the HF transmitters installed on Gulf's planes, and the dispatcher checked him inbound with a full load. About ten minutes had passed when Rob's voice came back on the radio, this time indicating a degree of tension: "Base, this is XUY. Get the Mounties to meet me on the dock. I got a crazy man aboard—tried to cut the tail off the aircraft with his chainsaw!"

Now, maybe that didn't get our attention. We all got up and peered

A Gulf Air Single Otter in flight over Quadra Island. Pilots referred to Gulf Air's airplanes as "green machines." It was joked that if you stood around for too long, you too would be painted in the owner's favourite colour.

KEN SWARTZ PHOTO

out the big window overlooking the docks. I don't know what we expected to see, because Rob was still at least five minutes away. Our chief pilot, Bob Pogue, got pretty excited about this and dashed down the stairs onto the dock. Nobody called the cops.

When XUY taxied up to the dock,

the passengers bailed out of the aircraft, all grinning and laughing. Seems our faller with the chainsaw had got a snootful of something and turned belligerent, possibly suicidal. He'd fired up his chainsaw and made for the big doors, managing to get one slightly ajar. He was about to buck into the

Workers from a logging camp in Rivers Inlet board a Gulf Air Beaver for a trip to Port Hardy. Loggers worked "ten in and four out," providing regular business for the airlines.

floor of the fuselage when two of his logger buddies grabbed and disarmed him.

The culprit was readily identifiable when he came walking down the dock carrying his 58-inch Pioneer saw, but Pogue couldn't figure out what to do about it and he certainly wasn't going to get physical with this tough little guy. Instead, he turned around and yelled up to the dispatch office, "Take this man's name. He'll never fly with us again!"

Everybody, including Rob, got a big kick out of that. Nobody got his name, and I suspect he went back into camp with us ten days later.

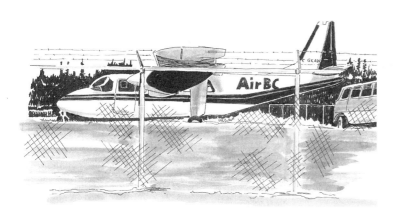

It was a BN2 Islander and it was looking very spiffy, having just been repainted in AirBC colours. The Pattison Group had just bought out six little coastal airlines and amalgamated them under the new name of AirBC. The new airline's paint shop at Vancouver airport had been working overtime to repaint a huge fleet of Beavers, Otters, Cessnas and light twin-engined aircraft, each appearing a little less clapped out in its new livery. This Islander, a "green machine" operated by Gulf Air's Port Hardy base, had just graduated to the fleet of the largest air carrier in the province.

Approach to Limits

The Islander wasn't the only dazzling thing on the Port Hardy tarmac this drizzly day. I was the picture of sartorial elegance in my newly issued AirBC uniform, complete with four gold bars halfway up to the elbow and a set of cast aluminum wings in the same paint job as the plane. Gone were the old workboots and blue jeans worn when flying for the previous management—we used to be bush pilots, but suddenly we were captains, no less. As such, we were required to stand closer to our razors in the mornings when we were attired in these spanking-new threads.

Seven passengers, all from one family, had chartered the Islander to Bella Coola to attend a family reunion. They filed past me into the aircraft, looking a little grim and apprehensive, while I was attempting to look more experienced than my uniform.

"Mother" was paying the bill and chose to sit beside me in the co-pilot seat. She had a very big handbag that she hung on the throttle levers while she fished inside it for something. The one daughter and five sons sprawled into the seats behind me and ignored my cabin announcement starting with "In the unlikely event." Mother interrupted me in mid-spiel: "I know I'm not supposed to smoke during take-off," she said, "but I am going to smoke the minute we have levelled off. I'm absolutely terrified of flying, but if I can smoke and have a little refreshment along the way, I can make it." Despite the absence of four bars on her sleeve, I got the picture: what Mother said, her family did; and, in that respect, she now considered me family. This all happened long ago— before smokers were required to step outside, and when the term "second-hand smoke" had not yet been coined.

Immediately after take-off Mother lit up, as did her six offspring in the back seats. She then unwrapped the brown paper from the object she had fished out of her handbag, a 26-ounce bottle of Drambuie. She spun the cap off and tossed it, with a grin, to somebody in the back seats, then threw back about a third of the bottle in one draft.

"Oh, that'll get me halfway there," she laughed. She took the cigarette from her mouth only to take a swig from the bottle—otherwise, the cigarette wagged from her lips as she spoke,

and she would close one eye against the sting of the rising smoke. From the back seats, six other cigarettes also wagged in unison, each adding to the growing obscuration in the cabin.

I have it on good authority that the human body generates 400 BTUs per hour. There were eight of us so generating, and you might say the humidity in the plane became very relative. The windshield and windows fogged up and ran with water. The only ventilation in this British-built airplane was an eight-inch square of the Plexiglas window beside the pilot. This little panel opened inward and, like most things of British design involving personal comfort, did nothing. The buildup of cigarette smoke and body heat became oppressive. While the weather report for the area called for five miles in rain, we were down to IFR (instrument flight rules) limits inside the cabin. When we passed Cape Caution, all seven of my passengers proceeded to butt out and light up another one. I put my foot down.

"No more smoking—please!"
Some foot!
"Oh, just this one! Please, please," Mother responded. "I just hate flying, and if I can't smoke I'll go crazy with fear."

I reluctantly acquiesced, and the six in the back assumed they too could

The author during his Gulf Air days (1979): the forest green pants of this uniform were hand-me-downs from a really skinny pilot. I had to walk slowly and sing soprano. The tie fit fine.

continue puffing. By the time we made it through the pass into Taleomey, the smoke from 14 cigarettes was trapped inside the Islander. I was nursing a beaner of a headache. When the plane's wheels barked on the concrete at Bella Coola, I was ready to pitch my biscuit.

This family of seven was met at Bella Coola airport by a five-passenger car, presumably driven by another relative. Jammed in as they were, all seven of them lit up as they drove off to their reunion. But I didn't notice whether Mother had taken her Drambuie. That question was answered later, when I found the empty bottle under the co-pilot seat. I left all the plane's doors open as I sat on the bench in front of the Wilderness Airlines office performing deep-breathing exercises. This went on for about half an hour before I got back into the Islander and returned to Port Hardy.

When I taxied the Islander into the big hangar at YZT, I noticed that the rain had made the new paint job a little grungy, and that the interior of the plane smelled like a cocktail bar on Sunday morning. But the plane had nothing on my fancy new uniform—it stank big time from that day forward, and I swear those four gold bars turned green with verdigris. I tossed the jacket in the baggage compartment and from then on wore only the pants of the uniform.

Over the years, those two pairs of pants performed yeoman service. When I retired from flying, both pairs were shiny in the backside but still serviceable. But the jacket continued to smell of stale smoke. I stripped it of its gold bars and presented it to the Salvation Army thrift shop. When I removed the gold stripes on the sleeve, a very faint trace of them was left on the blue worsted material.

Every time I pass someone wearing a navy blue blazer, I can't stop myself from checking out the arms. If I ever run into that jacket again, I think I'll step up and smell it.

Every Tuesday this prawn boat, located in Turnbull Cove north of Watson Island, produced 800 pounds of live prawns, which were picked up by a Beaver floatplane and flown to Port Hardy airport. At the airport, the prawns were loaded aboard a Boeing 737 jet for Vancouver. On one occasion, the liquid from one of the plastic tubs of prawns leaked into passengers' baggage on the Boeing. Thereafter, the commuter airline refused to carry live prawns. Sadly, the woman pictured at left with her ten-year-old son was killed in the crash of a Beaver flying in fog, only a few minutes after taking off from this cove in 1989.

52

3

A LITTLE HANGAR FLYING

Pilots' War Stories, Not Necessarily True

Voices from Within

Coastal seaplane pilots do not wear headphones, earphones or headsets; they wear David Clarks. That manufacturer's product is so popular with seaplane pilots that the name has become definitive. David Clarks are green and oval-shaped, with oil-filled ear cushions to mould to any head and ear shape—one size fits all. Inside those green ovals there are little speakers, and from those speakers the pilot of an amphibious Beaver performing a runway take-off from Vancouver airport, heading north for Port Hardy, will hear the tower advise him that he is "cleared from Whiskey for a Spanish departure." Fear not, the pilot's blood-alcohol reading is normal and there are no flamenco guitars accompanying his take-off—"Whiskey" is a runway intersection, and the "Spanish departure" is a northbound heading over the local beach at Spanish Banks.

Apart from receiving control tower and official messages, those David Clarks will also receive words on the company frequency informing the pilot on his way up the coast that a passenger is waiting to be picked up at Campbell River. Also from those green orbs, some pilot-to-pilot chit-chat, which is kept to a minimum because others are listening. But more than anything, silence—long periods of silence, in which only the somewhat reduced engine noise intrudes. Pilots live inside those David Clarks from take-off to landing, every single workday.

As I write, my David Clarks hang from a coat tree, as they have for several years now. Their nicks and scratches remind me of my glory days in Beaver, Otter and Cessna floatplanes tracking the splendid shorelines of the B.C. coast. The curly cord from the headset hangs vertically almost to the floor, and the little press-to-talk switch has not been pressed to talk for as many years now as when I wore them daily.

Hesitating, I take them down and, closing the door so others won't witness my insanity, don these old friends and loop the Velcro tab of the switch around my hand. Timidly at first, and with some apprehension, I press the little switch. Silence—the same silence that accompanied so many hours of

flight in the mid-coast area of Alert Bay, Port McNeill, Rivers Inlet and as far south as Campbell River. But then, suddenly, a voice. Is it just my mind playing tricks on me, or is there the slight background hiss of the radio carrier and some pilot from the past laughing and saying, "You'll never guess what happened to me on the sched today!" Many voices come tumbling into my ears from my old David Clarks.

There might have been more, but suddenly I feel something dripping down my neck. The oil from one of the ear pads is leaking onto my best shirt, attesting to the way of all flesh and David Clarks.

There is a Catch-22 situation when a young fledgling pilot tries to get work flying seaplanes on the B.C. coast. Operators won't hire a pilot without at least 1,000 hours on floats. So how does he get 1,000 hours if he can't get a job flying seaplanes? Nobody can afford to rent a seaplane for that many hours, so somehow the rules have to be bent. The usual route is for the beginner to get a job in northern Alberta, Saskatchewan or Ontario with a sport-fishing operation that is happy to let the

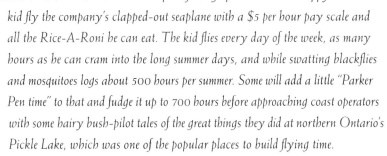

kid fly the company's clapped-out seaplane with a $5 per hour pay scale and all the Rice-A-Roni he can eat. The kid flies every day of the week, as many hours as he can cram into the long summer days, and while swatting blackflies and mosquitoes logs about 500 hours per summer. Some will add a little "Parker Pen time" to that and fudge it up to 700 hours before approaching coast operators with some hairy bush-pilot tales of the great things they did at northern Ontario's Pickle Lake, which was one of the popular places to build flying time.

Such experience sometimes leads to a dock boy's job with one of the coastal operators, gassing up airplanes and turning out Beavers off the dock at less than minimum wage, plus all the Cheezies he can eat, while waiting for the day the ops manager says: "Take this brat with you and let him fly the leg home when there are no passengers." Later that summer, this "brat" would be wearing Ray-Bans and tossing the odd bag of Cheezies to the other dock boys as they turn him out to fly the North Coast Sched.

I was a little older than those brats when I got my float endorsement and thought it might be a great way to earn a living. My solution to the 1,000 hours was also a little different.

Building Time

Buddy Recalma was a gentleman. In the real sense—a gentle man. He was the chief of the Qualicum Indian Band and the director of a Native organization known as the RAVEN Society, a.k.a. the Remote Area Video Educational Network. The organization's mission was to realize a single-sideband, high-frequency radio transmitter in all the remote Native villages on the coast, networked to a centre that would handle the day-to-day issues and requirements of these remote bands—a great concept, and one that was already in motion when I appeared on the scene selling electronic equipment to the society. Buddy purchased his first reel-to-reel videotape recorder to commence the video part of the program, which was set up to record the history of the various Native bands on the coast, particularly their unique tribal dances, using this then-new technology of reel-to-reel black-and-white video recorders and video cameras. Buddy and his wife, Diane, amassed miles of that half-inch videotape while recording the traditional dances of bands along the coast, from the Nass Valley on the Alaska border down to the Lower Mainland. Buddy asked me to help him edit these reels of tape, which, with some reluctance, I agreed to do. I have to admit that the many hours performing this work left me less than enamoured of watching Native dances, but the experience led to something much more to my liking.

"Why don't we buy a seaplane?" Buddy asked one day. "You could fly into the villages and install the single-sideband radios." It was a great idea, but I was not financially able to consider it. He persevered: "Find an airplane that

will do the job, and we can figure out how to pay for it later."

I did just that and came up with a Cessna 172 on floats that was owned by an industrial equipment company in Campbell River. They wanted $8,200 for the 1963 airplane, registered as CF-OQU. It was a pretty fair price. Buddy said, "Buy it. You can pay me back for half of it by a monthly payment that fits your wallet." These were great terms for me, and I agreed to pay for my half share at $200 per month.

I took delivery of OQU from Pat Finnerty, the seller's pilot, who assured me that the plane was in excellent shape. We went through the logbooks to establish that all the required maintenance records were in shape and up-to-date. Don Matheson, Island Airlines' chief pilot, took me up to Campbell Lake every day for about three weeks to teach me how to fly floats. He was the best thing that ever happened to me.

"Transport Canada requires only five hours' training for a float endorsement," Don said to me on the first day. "You're going to have 50 hours' training before I sign your logbook because this coast can eat the best of us, and a five-hour wonder hasn't got a chance."

He did just that and also took me on his airline flights around the coast, giving me control of the Beaver when

56

Loggers going into camp or fishermen rejoining their boats used seaplanes as city folk would hail cabs. Pictured are prawn fishermen returning to work at Turnbull Cove, ca. 1985.

there were no passengers aboard. We did figure-eight turns on the water on one float and then over onto the other; we took off in howling gales and in half-mile visibility; and he made me establish a line I would never cross in terms of weather, water conditions and loading. He emphasized fuel management and left me with a healthy respect for what I was getting into. One day he said, "Okay, see ya," and I loaded the plane with my radios and videotape recorders and took off for my first solo trip on floats to Prince Rupert—the farthest reach of the B.C. coast. On that trip I encountered every conceivable weather and water condition of which I had been warned, and I returned believing I was an ace. Later, I would learn the proper spelling of that word.

One day, Buddy phoned me. "I have to attend a funeral in Alert Bay," he said. "Will you fly me up?" It was

Fuel management is always a pilot's first consideration when travelling into the wilderness. Sullivan Bay was the traditional fuel source for piston-engine aircraft on the mid-coast. On those occasions when Sullivan ran out of avgas, Beaver pilots would use boat gas, which "seemed" to work fine. Cessnas and others were out of luck. This sign at Sullivan proved the need for a sense of humour when living in the rainforest.

ED PRICE DRAWING

58

a blustery day but clear to the blue. "Sure thing," I said, and we agreed to meet at Long Lake in Nanaimo, where I was keeping the airplane. We took off at noon and headed up the island. We were flying into a hard westerly, and the little plane was getting hammered. Buddy is the skipper of a 60-foot seine boat, and I didn't think the turbulence would bother him, but as we came abeam his own home at Qualicum Bay we were bouncing around pretty bad.

"This airplane's too small," he said. "Land at Deep Bay and let me out. I've had enough." That was the first and last time he flew in the plane. I ultimately paid him out for the whole airplane and flew it for the next four years up and down the coast, selling electronic parts and equipment.

When I started the airline operation for the owner of Aquila Air out of Shawl Bay, my time was a bit shy of 1,000 hours on floats. Later, when joining Gulf Air, I was pushing 3,000 hours and still trying not to cross that imaginary line I had set for myself. So much for Pickle Lake. No Rice-A-Roni for this guy.

An ELT is an emergency locator transmitter. It is a yellow box measuring about ten inches high and three inches wide, and it connects on top to the aircraft's special antenna mounted on the aft section of the plane's fuselage. ELTs are powered by self-contained batteries and are designed to send an unmistakable signal on the emergency frequency when an impact with a G-force of seven sets them off. They work pretty well despite being a source of much concern for authorities, who fret about the batteries either blowing up or just dying from old age. Spurious ELT signals are not unheard of. Often, they are set off by mistake—if you drop an ELT, guess what? Also, they have been known to go off on their own in aircraft sitting for long periods of time in hot sunshine. Because of these false alarms, before search action takes place there is generally a great deal of running around and phoning people. Not so in this case, as there was an alert out for an overdue aircraft.

On Being Professional

"It was raining like hell and between the big fat raindrops, snowflakes the size of saucers." That's how it was described to me by a pilot friend who was there that day. We were talking about Port Hardy airport on a day back in January 1978.

An Islander belonging to an outfit called Tradewinds had just touched down on runway 25 and was taxiing in to the gas pit. The runway visibility was no more than a quarter mile in this deluge, and the pilot would be having a hard time finding those little blue lights at the intersection. This light twin had departed Prince Rupert, on an instrument flight plan, and was headed to Vancouver with a fuel stop at Port Hardy.

The pilot and five passengers got out at the fuel bay, and the passengers immediately bolted for the safety of the terminal. The pilot wasn't so lucky. He climbed up onto the wing and accepted the gas nozzle from the fuel attendant. When he removed the gas cap, the pilot put his glove over the filler pipe to keep the rain out of the tank. He hunched himself over against the downpour and tried, vainly, to hurry the gas going into the tank. When it was full, he capped the tank and crossed over to the other wing, where he did the same things, then handed the hose to the attendant. He got down and walked over to the terminal building, where one of his passengers had bought him a cup of coffee.

"How do you know where you're going in this stuff?" asked one of the men.

"Oh, it's all done with numbers," he replied, laughing.

They all got back into the airplane, and the pilot started the engines. He taxied the aircraft along the intersection to the active runway, and then stopped, holding short of the runway.

On the instrument panel of this Islander there were two transceivers. The top one was showing the frequency for Port Hardy FSS (Flight Service Station), and having selected that radio, the pilot requested that his flight plan be re-opened for the continuing flight to Vancouver. The Port Hardy FSS controller had received specific approvals from Vancouver Centre for this aircraft and read off these instructions carefully. These instructions were read back by the pilot exactly as he had received them, to which the FSS station replied, "Your read-back is correct. You are cleared for immediate take-off." This clearance was followed by those exact instructions as to what altitude the aircraft was to climb to, what Victor airways he was to follow, and where and when he was to report to Vancouver Centre. Sufficient to say, the instructions ensured that the required separation between aircraft travelling on the airways system was maintained. It was the pilot's responsibility to do precisely what was detailed in this flight plan. Our pilot did exactly that when he took off and climbed through this blowing rain and snow and broke out into clearer skies between two cloud layers. It didn't matter that he could now see ahead; he was flying on instruments, and his eyes were scanning the flight panel in the prescribed method he had learned a few years back when he first studied for his instrument rating.

While maintaining his selected frequency on the Port Hardy FSS, the pilot spun the tuning knobs on the second radio to 121.5 MHz, which is the distress frequency. This is not a mandatory procedure but is good practice, because in the event of trouble he could get a message off immediately, and should someone else be in trouble, he would hear their transmissions and could relay messages. In flight at 8,000 feet the Islander was, in effect, an 8,000-foot antenna. On this day our pilot's choice of procedures would save a life.

Immediately after he tuned in to the distress frequency, an ELT signal burst into his earphones. He was momentarily electrified by the dreaded sound, then sprang into action: he switched radios and radioed back to Port Hardy that he had a signal on one-two-one-decimul-fiyive." (That's how he pronounced it, which is how it's done to avoid confusion.)

Back at the FSS station, the controller on duty turned up the volume on his 121.5 receiver. He could not hear a signal and advised the Islander accordingly. The pilot replied that he had a strong signal from the ELT and that he would be prepared to home in on that signal and report back an exact geographic position. Vancouver Centre was advised, and the Islander was cleared from its IFR planned route to proceed at its own discretion to home in on the emergency signal. A nice piece of flying under nasty conditions brought the Islander directly over the ELT transmission. The pilot performed three homing procedures on the signal

and came up with what is referred to as a "cocked hat," in the centre of which was the exact position of whomever or whatever was transmitting the distress signal. The pilot of the Islander radioed this information to Port Hardy FSS, who, in turn, advised the Comox search and rescue (SAR) squadron. Comox had a Buffalo aircraft in the air coming home from the B.C. interior. That aircraft was carrying a para-rescue team and had been proceeding by a Fraser Canyon route when it was diverted to the lat and long (latitude and longitude) position provided by the Islander. It took the Buffalo 45 minutes to arrive over what was now determined to be a crash site.

It was a dismal situation for the Buffalo crew: the weather prevented them from performing a visual reconnaissance of the site. The SAR team had to rely entirely on the position established by the Islander. There had been an aircraft reported overdue on a flight in this vicinity, so they were fairly certain that their help was needed. They did what they are trained to do—they jumped blind through the overcast: a jumpmaster and his green trainee on his first "live" jump onto a real target. The Buffalo dropped the two men at the lowest possible altitude. Their descent was rapid and the landing hard and, unfortunately, into a

A typical float camp. One family lived here, at Shawl Bay, for some 30 years. Not everyone would enjoy the lifestyle, but a life in the rainforest takes one far from the madding crowd.

stand of timber. The trainee made it, the jumpmaster broke his ankle, but the two were directly on target. The wreckage of a Cessna 185 floatplane was sighted and its pilot saved from near death by the expert actions of that young, so-called "green" jumper, who also set his boss's ankle and got the two patients onto the rescue boat.

The pilot of the Islander? He flew on to Vancouver, where he discharged his passengers, put the plane in the hangar and went home to his wife and two kids. His wife had put in a heavy day with the young children, so he looked after them, reading them a story before bed. He can't remember the name of the TV show he watched that night before hitting the sack himself.

There were three Native villages in the area. The largest was Kingcome and the smallest a little place called Hopetown, where 12 members of the same extended family resided. They boarded the sched flight frequently, travelling on a warrant from the provincial medical health service, ostensibly to see the doctor at Port McNeill or Alert Bay. Often, it was as much a grocery run as a medical reason that prompted their flight, but the trip described here was truly one of a kind.

Man in the Box

I had hauled a load of groceries and one passenger into Nimmo Bay Resort, flying a Beaver on straight floats. It was a hot day, and the sun, beating on the metal fuselage, had warmed up the plane's interior considerably. I was busy off-loading the groceries when a soft voice addressed me from the vicinity of the aircraft's tail.

"Nice day, Jack."

I stopped what I was doing and looked around to find Henry standing by the tail. Henry Speck, from nearby Hopetown Village, the finest carver in the area.

"Hey, Henry, what are you doing here at Nimmo Bay?" To which he grinned sheepishly. Henry had a well-developed sense of humour, and I could see the twinkle in his eye as he answered my question.

"I slept here on the dock last night—I wasn't too welcome at home."

Not quite the typical float camp, Nimmo Bay Resort is pictured here in a sketch made by the author in 1982, before the lodge became the premier wilderness destination for the international jet set. Owners Craig and Deborah Murray invented the heli-fishing concept, which brought the world to their doorstep.

64

JACK SCHOFIELD '89

"On the dock? That must have been uncomfortable. Why are you in trouble at home?"

"We had a little party, and I did some mischief—cut all the antennas down on the roof. TV and telephone reception not up to much now. Elsie was very unhappy."

Elsie was the chief of the Hopetown band, and she was also Henry's mother-in-law. I would not want to have cut down Elsie's antennas.

"I was wondering if I could thumb a ride with you to Port McNeill, Jack," said my friendly miscreant.

I explained to Henry that my next stop was at Hopetown, where I was picking up Elsie and Julie, her daughter,

Henry's wife.

"I'm flying them to Port McNeill, Henry. My guess is you wouldn't want to face them at this time?" I came to that conclusion as I watched Henry's expression turn to horror at the thought of such a confrontation. Henry became silent as he digested that piece of news, and I finished unloading the groceries. As I was about to close the big passenger door, he stopped the door and pointed to the little baggage compartment behind the rear sling seat.

"I could ride in there, Jack. They wouldn't know I was there."

The baggage compartment is a tin box measuring about 30 inches square. It is completely hidden by the rear seat,

The dock at Hopetown Village. Hopetown was the traditional home of only 12 people. This photo catches an Orca Air Beaver, AQX, during a potlatch at the village in 1984. Several years later, AQX crashed into the water while flying in fog not far from Hopetown. The plane and its three occupants were never found.

which is a sling or hammock made of black Naugahyde.

"Henry, you can't ride in that box. It's too small even for a short guy like you. And it will be hotter'n hell in there." Henry wasn't listening. He was crawling into the box, and darned if he didn't double himself up and with a big grin declare that it was like first-class Air Canada.

Reluctantly, I agreed to his caper and hung up the sling seat, concealing him in his chosen compartment. We took off for Hopetown—a three-minute flight.

Elsie and Julie were on the dock, waiting. When they got into the plane, they did something they had never done before—they both sat in the back sling seat. Usually, Elsie took the co-pilot seat beside me, with Julie on the bench seat behind. But on this occasion they each plopped right down on the Naugahyde at the back, not more than half an inch between them and their son-in-law/husband/mischief-maker. It took all I had to keep from bursting out in laughter.

The flight to Port McNeill took about 15 minutes. The two women de-planed, booked me to pick them up in three hours and commenced their walk up the dock to the townsite. I dropped the sling seat, and Henry emerged,

The welcoming totem at Hopetown Village provides a backdrop for some of the village's principal residents, posing for the author in 1985: left to right, Henry Speck; his wife, Julie; her mother, Henry's mother-in-law and also the band chief, Elsie Williams; and Elsie's son, Charlie.

very hot, but none the worse for wear. We had a good laugh, so good that we didn't notice the two women returning to the plane, believing they had left a bag on board. They were astounded to see Henry, and he was alarmed to see them. A very long moment ensued.

Then Elsie's thunder-dark face suddenly lightened. To my great relief, we all broke into gales of laughter.

My last sight of them was as a threesome strolling arm in arm up the dock. I guessed they were on their way to buy a new TV antenna.

The captain of an airliner never sees his passengers during the flight, particularly in this day and age, when a locked, bulletproof door secures the airliner's flight deck. In a Beaver or Otter seaplane, however, the pilot and passengers share a common space, much like in a car. The seaplane pilot gets to know something about each passenger. For instance, on one particularly bumpy trip, a big, burly logger, seated beside me, threw up from the effect of the turbulence while a skinny librarian-type in the back seat got a real kick out of being thrown around in the sky. Then there was the passenger who had once taken some flying lessons and wanted to try flying the plane. Much to his surprise, I transferred the yoke over to him and told him to fill his boots. We were high enough that I could correct any problem he got into, and there were no other passengers aboard. He did fine, except that he couldn't seem to maintain altitude and the plane kept descending. I told him to hold the nose on the horizon. The plane still kept descending, and when I looked over at him, I was astonished to see him with his head back holding his nose on the horizon.

Here's a story about four passengers I really got to know and, hopefully, will never chance to meet in a dark alley.

Down in the Mouth North of 60: The Root Canal from Hell

Before heading into the bush to fly for a remote fishing lodge located far north of La Ronge, Saskatchewan, and just north of latitude 60, I thought it a good idea to see a dentist. The dentist agreed: "You'll never find anyone up there in the boondocks to perform this kind of work," he exclaimed. For the hour that he had my mouth clamped open, he regaled me with an endless description of the root canal he was performing. I hate dentists who explain what they are doing to me. How could I have guessed that my first flight for that fishing lodge was to take four New York dentists into a remote lake in search of lake trout and northern pike? As things turned out, any one of those four dentists would gladly have performed major dental surgery on me—pulling one tooth at a time, without anaesthetic, and describing the event in great detail, with relish.

There was ice fog on the water when I awoke that first morning at Kasba Lake. Doug Hill, the lodge owner, explained that it would burn off in a couple of hours and would start reforming around four in the afternoon as the temperature dropped. He warned me to get back to the lodge before it socked in. I took off at 10:30 in the morning with the four dentists, two guides and one 75-horse Mercury outboard. We flew up Kasba Lake for 50 miles and then turned inland to our destination—a lake where the lodge had stashed a 14-foot tin boat in the bush for the winter. We found that lake still frozen solid—it was only May 12 and breakup was late, so I couldn't land. It was decided that we would land on the river flowing out of the lake and drop the two guides off on the river bank. They would hoof it up to the frozen lake and bring the boat down the rapids to the Beaver, which I would beach on a gravel bar in mid-river.

(Seems to me that sport fishermen and hunters create monstrous situations just so they can hook or shoot something.)

The dentists and I waited in the Beaver for about an hour as an increasingly heavy rain drummed on the wings and the windows, which were fogging up from the high humidity joining forces with our combined body heat. These New Yorkers had never been in an airplane before—that is, a real airplane, like a Beaver. Nor had they ever travelled too far from Park Avenue. They were just agog at what was happening. I didn't let on that so was I.

When the guides finally loaded the dental corps aboard the boat to go fishing, I warned them to be back at 3:30 so that we could beat the fog back to the lodge. They returned an hour late, at 4:30, and before we could get airborne, the ice fog had engulfed us and obscured the entire river—a take-off was out of the question. Not a happy situation. The guides advised that there was a small cabin on the shore built for just such an emergency. We made the aircraft fast to the gravel bar before taking the boat upriver to the cabin. Before leaving the aircraft, I transmitted on 128.85, a corporate frequency: "Anybody on this frequency?"

A big voice boomed back, identifying itself as an airliner at 30,000 feet, en route someplace and happy to help:

"What can we do for you?" I explained our situation, requesting that they get word to the lodge that we were okay and that we would return first thing in the morning. I learned later that the airliner had advised Saskatoon FSS (Flight Service Station), who looked up our Beaver's ident in their book of words and phoned the listed owner 2,000 miles away in Parksville, B.C., who, in turn, telephoned the lodge on satellite phone to advise that we were okay but grounded for the night. The weather was against us, but technology was on side.

We made off in the boat to find the emergency shelter, and when we got there we realized that our message to the airliner wasn't entirely correct—we weren't okay. The emergency shelter was a mere ten feet square, had a dirt floor and provided no source of heat for these seven thoroughly soaked, shivering and bedraggled individuals. When the guides decided to chop a hole in the roof (it worked in those Indian teepees, didn't it?) and light a fire on the floor, the resulting smoke drove us all to our knees, sucking fresh air from any crack in the boards we could find. This proved to be the longest night in history. I have never met four people so far out of their element as those dental surgeons from New York City.

During the flight back to home base the next morning, there was total silence aboard the aircraft. There was more of it when we joined the happy campers at breakfast in the lodge. I didn't envy the first patients of those dentists when they resumed their practice back in Manhattan: "Open wide. You won't believe what happened to me." That would be the root canal from hell. What really amused me was that these dentists paid big bucks for the experience.

More adventures awaited me in this frozen land. I realized that I had been spoiled by flying the B.C. coast, with its mountainous topography. This northern territory seemed featureless and without navigational aids. One had to map-read assiduously, as there was nothing obvious to steer by and the compass was no less than 35 degrees out of whack because of the proximity of the North Pole. "Not true," said a local pilot who had spent his life in the area I'd called featureless. "D'ya see that lake over there that looks like a dog humping a football? When you get to it, you will be able to see another lake resembling [I will leave his anatomical comparison to your imagination] and then over there a lake the shape of Marilyn Monroe's ..." I got the drift, and over the next three months I found my way around by making up my own descriptions of the zillions of little unnamed lakes that appeared with the Arctic thaw.

After three months in the area, I figured I was an ace, and on a day near the end of my contract, landed on a lake the shape of a—well, you don't want to know. I laid the aircraft alongside a bank of solid granite, where a survey team had constructed a little raft. It was a very hot day. I was quick to open the pilot's door, and I held it open with my foot as the prop windmilled to a stop. My headset came off in a hurry because, in this heat, it was burning my ears. My glasses caught on the headphones and spun out the door, arcing in what seemed like slow motion into the crystal-clear water of the lake. Four men standing on the dock witnessed the mishap and peered into the water, watching my glasses perform a falling-leaf descent into the depths. The water was so clear that we could see my bifocals come to rest on a little ledge on the granite wall at an unknown depth below the surface. It was a catastrophe—I needed those glasses in order to fly and map-read in this unforgiving land.

One of the men on the dock took his clothes off. Just like that—he stripped naked and dove into the near-frozen water. We all watched him, aghast at the man's bravery. He appeared to be turning blue with the cold as he descended into the clear water. He didn't make it. He came to the surface breaking water with hardly a splash, and mounted the dock with little apparent effort or concern. His body resembled that of a Greek god, a blue Greek god.

"How deep do you figure?" somebody yelled.

"Maybe 30 feet," was the reply as he dove once more into the frigid water—water that had been solid Arctic ice only a month before.

This time, we could see he was going to reach the little ledge, as his dive had given him the required momentum. He reached out and grasped the glasses, and then, with one kick, he rose to the surface, mounted the dock, walked over to me and handed me the glasses. Wordlessly, he turned and climbed the rock face to the grass field above and walked, almost casually, to his tent.

Somebody said, "Talk about cool. And I don't mean the water!"

The diver didn't emerge from the tent until we flew out. On the flight back to base, I figured I'd better get one of those little strings that clip onto the glasses and go around your neck. I didn't have the desire or the physique for the Polar Bear Olympics.

Pilots enjoy a sense of omniscience when flying over the earth: on a clear day the view seems to be forever, and from a few hundred feet, cities and towns appear clean and orderly. Mountains are magnificent when approached, and their peaks are awesome, often forbidding, when flown over. A hidden lake will suddenly reveal itself with a sparkle of reflected sunlight. Who could not feel God-like, seeing his own shadow cast against a cloud, encircled in its own private rainbow?

The Dog Who Owned the World

The entrance to the terminal was unlocked, so someone was up and around, but there was no one in sight. The click of the door latch echoed through the empty terminal as he walked past the baggage carousel, his footsteps resounding in the large open space. A solitary duffle bag sat alone on the conveyor belt. He wondered how someone could have forgotten a bag like that; he picked it up and continued across the vacant room, taking a key from his pocket and unlocking the "Staff Only" door. Immediately, there was a sense of suspended animation: the airline dispatch desk was strewn with papers; the transceiver, purposely left on standby, was making little hissing noises to itself, its glowing red jewel reflecting on the white canvas of the duffle bag as he set it on the desk.

Out of the corner of his eye he could see empty baggage carts in the freight room. He walked past them into the pilots' ready room with its one wall entirely papered with *Playboy* centrefolds. The headset that had the individual volume controls for each ear was hanging among the other earphones on the rack, and he chose that one without hesitation. He then walked through the steel freight door and into the paved alleyway behind the building. As he locked the door behind him, he could see OCQ parked at the gas pumps on the tarmac at the end of the alley. The Beaver amphibian would be loaded with groceries, and if he was lucky, the last ramp rat of yesterday would have filled the front and centre tanks. That proved to be the case, so he didn't have to pump the gas. But there was a surprise after all: Perky was tied to the float strut and was lying on a mat.

He knew the dog's name because there was a cardboard note taped to the gas pumps telling him to drop off the poodle, with the groceries, at Scott Cove. A mat had been laid out beside the pontoon for the dog to sleep on, and a dish of dog food had been left for him. The food dish had moved beyond the dog's reach. The dog sat up and looked at him with very big brown eyes that seemed to be trusting, if a little bewildered. He moved cautiously toward the dog until he had determined the animal's disposition. Perky just sat there—no wag of the tail, just a questioning look.

He picked up the food dish and moved it closer, but still the dog didn't move.

There was a three-step boarding stair pushed up to the pontoon. He would have to make the dog climb that before lifting him into the cabin. He thought it had been a dumb decision to leave the dog here unattended. Untying the leash from the strut, he led the dog up the stairs. He then put one arm under the dog's rear end and the other arm under its chest and lifted the animal into the cabin, where it just lay down on the floor beside the groceries. Those big brown eyes followed him as he closed the door.

He returned to the tarmac, rolled up the mat and stuffed it into the baggage compartment. Then he placed the food dish in the cabin beside the dog and went down the steps again. He did his walkaround of the aircraft, looking carefully at everything before pushing the stairs out of the way and jumping up on the pontoon.

The sky was like smoke—white smoke. He couldn't tell with any assurance just how high a ceiling it was, but visibility was forever under the early morning cloud cover. He could see Numas Island offshore and knew it to be 17 miles away. Looking through the

72

dew-covered windshield made everything look distorted, but that would disappear with the first blast from the prop. He pumped the primer, flicked on the master switch and engaged the starter. When four blades had passed his eyes, he snapped the two mag switches on, and the 985 coughed into life—wonderful engine.

Perky got up and put both feet on the flap lever between the front seats and trained those big browns on him. He patted the co-pilot seat, and the dog leapt onto the seat and looked out the now clear windshield. His tongue came out and stayed out for a couple of deep breaths. The cowling jiggled a little from the vibrations of the big engine as the throttle was advanced. The toe brakes were used, alternately, to steer them out of the fuel bay and into the taxiway. The pilot taxied right out onto the big white numbers indicating that this runway pointed to zero seven zero degrees magnetic. There he sat for several moments, gazing down the long runway to the steel grey ocean and occasionally checking the oil temperature gauge. Those big browns were on him again when he opened the throttle and, holding the toe brakes on, switched one magneto off and on, and then the other, and cycled the propeller into full-course pitch then back to fine. The poodle was very curious about that—it

probably didn't notice that there was no excessive mag drop and temperatures were now in the green.

The white dotted line on the runway sped under the belly, and the many cracks in the concrete thumped the main wheels, which protruded from the bottom of the pontoons. To save them from this pounding, the little wheels at the front end of the pontoons were held off the runway during the take-off run. Perky was seated now, seemingly checking the instrument panel as the rumbling noise suddenly stopped. The pilot looked at the dog as he slowly pumped a lever close to the dog's nose. The dog looked back, and then turned away to look out the side window at the trees flashing by.

He stayed low because he knew that dogs' ears were sensitive to altitude—dogs and young babies would either whine or cry when their ears popped from altitude. When they came abeam of the island, he could see right over the 15 or so miles to the mainland and could pick out the entrance to the channel. The sea was very flat and the air calm. Perky was taking in the magnificent beauty of the rainforest as they entered the inlet and tracked the shoreline into the complex of waterways. The inlets intersected like streets and avenues, and the dog took particular notice of any sign of life that they passed—Sullivan Bay caught his attention as that watering hole came alongside. Ahead, an island the exact shape of a haystack marked the path down the inlet. To the right of Stackhouse Island, a little channel wound its way into a bay and to a group of houses—one with a red roof.

Perky seemed to take in each of the scenes as the two flew into a narrows called Pomfrey's and came into a wide sound named for a famous British warship of Captain Cook's time. He almost told this fact to the dog, but stopped himself and shook his head at his ridiculous reaction to the animal. When he turned back into the cockpit, the dog was looking at him—still wondering what was going on, he thought. Crossing the sound, they passed over a couple of islands named the Burdwood Group, but he couldn't tell the dog why they were named that. As they entered the cove, however, he spoke aloud to the poodle—facetiously, of course. "This is Scott Cove, Perky: your master will be waiting for you." He didn't explain that Captain Vancouver, who had charted these waters, named the cove after one of his officers, or that Francis Point, which they had passed, was named by Cook after a seaman who had shot a deer there from a longboat. The deer had fallen into the water, and Thomas Point was named for the other seaman who had jumped in, swum to it and got it into the boat for the crew's dinner that night.

He and Perky had owned the world for 35 minutes, from the moment he had loaded the poodle at the terminal back at the airport. He and the brown-eyed dog had owned the sky and sea and the cedars and firs blurring by as they had banked and turned in the magnificent waterways with the rising hills on each shore. Their joint proprietorship of this early morning world had lasted into the mouth of Scott Cove, at which point a click came through the headphones and abruptly ended his and the dog's adventure.

"Good morning, OCQ. Where are you?"

"Just landing Scott Cove," he said into his boom microphone. The dog cocked its head, wondering whom he was talking to.

"Was Perky okay? You got him okay?"

"Best co-pilot I ever had."

The dispatcher's metallic voice said, "Yeah, poodles are smart. Check you landing Scott Cove—wheels up."

"Gear up," he said as he and Perky touched down, the pontoons creating long ruts in the glassy morning waters of the pristine little cove.

ART COX

A pilot friend of mine once flew as a stand-in co-pilot on a plane owned by the great musician Ray Charles. When he was introduced to the blind pianist in the cockpit of the celebrity's DC-3, my friend was surprised when Charles reached out and ran his hands all over the co-pilot's face. Ray explained, with his trademark grin, that this was his way of knowing what someone looked like.

One of the celebrities mentioned in the following story didn't show up for the flight. The one who did has not been identified by name, in case the story might prove embarrassing.

Celebrity Flight: A Day with a Guru

"'Take Me Home, Country Roads'—that's my favourite song." This from James, the older, more experienced pilot who many suspected was the dispatcher's pet because he seemed to get all the choice flights.

"'Annie's Song' was his best," said the other pilot, who had drawn the short straw.

"Sing whatever song you like, you guys, but you"—and the dispatcher pointed at the one whom we will refer to as the lesser pilot—"have got the guru, and James here gets John Denver."

We didn't get to fly many celebrities in this airline, but today a well-known guru was arriving at Port Hardy with his entourage and had chartered a flight into Cracroft Island—to a rarely used little bay on this island on the west side of Johnstone Strait. The famous pop singer John Denver was to arrive later and fly in to join the spiritual leader and other followers, who were already camped on the island.

"You like jazz, so you probably could stand some spiritual guidance, while I'm big-time country," James declared. "So I deserve to fly John Denver." He grinned.

The guru arrived with two followers, right on time. The three men all wore what I would describe as flowing robes—black and hanging right down to the ground. The great man himself had a reel-to-reel Sony video recorder slung over his shoulder and was poking the camera at everyone and everything that interested him. The three men were carrying on an animated conversation in another language—Tibetan, was our lesser pilot's guess as they augered down Johnstone Strait in the Beaver. The destination was in sight when the radio blared in the pilot's ear—it was dispatch telling them that John Denver had called, that he was detained and would be arriving tomorrow. He would fly to the island direct from Vancouver, so we wouldn't be flying him.

"Hey, James, you've just been taken down that country road," the lesser pilot gleefully replied into the boom mic. He then turned and addressed the passengers in English to give them the message. They were a very happy group and didn't seem to mind just when John Denver was to arrive.

The Beaver landed in the little bay on East Cracroft and taxied toward the beach, where several brightly coloured tents could be seen pitched among the trees. From a previous trip into this bay, the pilot knew that he would bottom onto soft sand long before he could reach the shore. He spotted a large crowd gathered on shore and headed toward them.

Before the pontoons hit the sand, the pilot swung the craft around to point out of the bay in the direction of his planned take-off. He then lifted the water rudders and dropped 45 degrees of flap, allowing the plane to sail backward with the wind. The Beaver did not go far before coming to a stop on a sandbar. Immediately, the crowd on the beach commenced wading toward the plane. As they got closer, the pilot noted that some of them were stark naked—in fact, most of them were starkers. When they got to the plane, four of them carried the laughing guru on their shoulders to shore—it was quite a sight. Then the other two men on the plane were carried ashore in the same manner. A very lovely, well-endowed young woman asked the pilot if he wanted to come ashore.

"I'd love to, but I have to go back to work," was his grinning reply as he

Beaver JOM was a perennial: it showed up in different colours in its many years of flying the coast. When this photo was taken, in 1983, JOM was owned by Orca Air and had just landed a group of celebrities at Nimmo Bay.

waved and cranked the engine into life. The aircraft refused to budge from its sandy roost. He gunned the engine, making lots of noise and blowing water on those standing behind—all to no avail. He shut down the engine and called out to the naked young woman, explaining that if some of them could rock the aircraft while he gunned the engine, the pontoons would likely break free of the sand. Four women came to the rescue and commenced rocking the plane from the stern of the floats. The beauty just stood and observed, smiling and waving. It worked, and the plane broke free. They

all waved, and he waved back. When he got into the air, he thought a flypast was in order and did a low and over, wagging his wings at the women as they waded ashore.

"Well, did you get some spiritual guidance?" James asked when the lesser pilot returned from the flight.

"I learned to transcend earthly desires," he replied. "And I have changed my taste in music. I'm into rock—heavy rock."

James didn't get the joke and was ticked off that he didn't get to meet John Denver.

Corporate aircraft are a common feature of the coastal aviation scene. Forest companies, logging contractors, equipment suppliers and utility companies require the convenience of sending their own aircraft into remote camps and installations. The B.C. Telephone Company, in its day, employed an amphibious Turbo Beaver, C-FASA, out of Port Hardy airport. This airplane served the company's many remote repeater stations along the coast. The company pilots rotated their flying duties between a Cessna Citation bizjet out of Vancouver and this pretty little bush plane serving the mid and north coast territories.

Stand-in Pilot

Tailbummer Joe

Vacations had upset the regular schedule. The B.C. Telephone Company pilot, scheduled for his regular turn at Port Hardy flying the turbine-powered Beaver, was on a beach somewhere in Hawaii.

"You will be flying for B.C. Tel this week," said Villi Douglas, AirBC's base manager at Port Hardy. He was pointing to me.

"Moi?" I replied. "Flying that beautiful Turbo Beaver?"

"Not a chance," said Villi. "You get OCQ."

OCQ was a nice Beaver, but nothing like ASA, the telephone company's state-of-the-art bush plane that was fitted with every electronic bell and whistle devised by man.

Shafts of sunlight penetrating a rainstorm—just one of the natural phenomena pilots experience when flying the coast. Pictured here is a Turbo Beaver amphibian, C-FASA, climbing out of Keith Anchorage.

Nevertheless it was an enjoyable week, lacking the pressures of my regular flying duties, and the passengers—installation technicians maintaining the company's remote repeater stations along the coast—were pleasant and interesting. We did flights into such places as Bella Coola and Keith Anchorage in Kwakshua Channel, and some local trips into Sullivan Bay and Wakeman Sound. On my second-last day, the crew of four were headed up to Bella Bella. This flight would become memorable for one particular member of that crew.

It was a warm day with a light westerly breeze. The Beaver's cabin was a happy place, with casual conversation between friends as we trucked up Fitz Hugh Sound. I was included in the crew's banter, as we had all grown to know each other during the week's flights, and when we landed at Bella Bella they all gave me the raspberry for a greased-on landing in the bay. The seaplane dock at Bella Bella is quite long, and on this occasion it was completely empty, so I laid the aircraft alongside about halfway down toward the shore end. The crew got out and sat on the step rungs to change into their workboots and gird up with their tool pouches for the job ahead. I bid them all goodbye and agreed to pick them up at three o'clock that afternoon. As the sea was calm and the wind favoured my straight-out departure, I just pushed the nose of the floats off the dock, jumped in, flashed up the engine and taxied away from the dock. Then, as all systems were go, I took off straight out of the bay.

When OCQ returned at three, the crew were waiting for me—all smiles and laughter. I was, seemingly, the butt of their laughter and was confused until they explained.

"Ed here was bending down, tying his boots with his butt facing your tailplane," explained one of the laughing installers. "When you taxied away, the tailplane caught him on the backside and dumped him into the water. You should have seen his face!" They all laughed at the recollection—even Ed, who had spent the day working in wet clothes because of his unexpected swim in the saltchuck.

The regular pilot returned the next week, and I went back to flying the sched—I'm sure the installation guys were glad things were back to normal.

An Oily Episode

A popular saying suggests that bad things happen in threes, but comedian George Carlin said, "Things happen in ones." I had one more funny/odd event take place when standing in for a vacationing corporate pilot.

They called him "Beaver Bob," and he flew an amphibious Beaver called IPL, which was owned by a major forest company with several logging camps in the mid-coast area. Beaver Bob was a nice guy, but he rarely smiled and he seemed to take life very seriously. Flight safety, for example, was a big thing with Bob. No one would argue with his concern, but he was prone to judging other pilots acerbically if they, in his opinion, transgressed his own rules. So I was surprised and somewhat honoured when he asked that I be assigned to fly his airplane during his vacation. The job involved much the same kind of flying as I was doing with the airline—taking workers and supplies into camps. One difference was the extended standby at the camps, waiting for the crew change. I must have gained a few pounds from long hours of sampling the cookhouse fare at the Scott Cove, Kingcome and Drury Inlet camps.

On my last day, a lady I will call Betty arrived at the company offices at Port Hardy airport. Betty was a camp cook, and she had long refused to fly—she was terrified of flying. The company usually took her in and out of camp using the company speedboat. On this day the speedboat was out of service and she was needed in Kingcome. Somebody talked her into taking the plane this one time—*Please, Betty.* She agreed, but was filled with trepidation, and she told me so before we took off from the runway at Port Hardy. I assured her that the flight would be a piece of cake and that we would be in Kingcome in 20 minutes.

It was not all that nice a day, as the southeast wind was gusting and the winds aloft were quite high, with the upper clouds moving pretty quickly. Down at 800 feet, where we fly, it was bumpy but nothing to write home about. Betty froze into the co-pilot seat beside me as I bantered away, trying to keep her mind occupied.

The de Havilland Beaver has an oil filler spout right in the cockpit. It is located between the pilot and co-pilot seats at floor level. The cap on the oil filler is painted yellow and is designed to twist on and lock much like a car's gas cap. Unknown to me, Betty had kicked the oil cap; it had come undone and oil had been puking out into the co-pilot's footwell since shortly after take-off. Betty was wearing flip-flops, with her bare toes protruding. The

very hot oil was burning Betty's toes, but she said nothing—she was frozen with fear. As we entered Fife Sound, I smelled something and discovered the loose cap and about two quarts of hot oil in Betty's footwell. Her eyes were like saucers, staring at me in terror. "I was afraid to tell you," she stammered as I replaced the cap and checked the oil pressure—still normal, but the engine would be down at least two quarts, and Beavers like oil.

The footwell is quite a deep indentation in the Beaver floor and has two little holes at the bottom to allow water to exit onto the aircraft's belly. The oil was now finding its way out of these holes and spraying down the belly of Beaver Bob's much-pampered pristine Beaver, and maybe the engine was about to seize up for want of oil. I called dispatch and advised them that I was having a minor problem and would be landing at Sullivan Bay, just two minutes away.

"How's Betty doing?" replied Maureen, the company's dispatcher.

"She's well oiled," I replied, much to Maureen's confusion.

When I docked at Sullivan, Pat Finnerty came out to greet us on the fuel dock.

"You've got a problem," he said, eyeing the dripping fuselage, which was now smeared with oil from stem

to gudgeon. He heard my story with amusement, then handed me two replacement cans of oil and a six-pack of paper towels. Betty stood on the dock wringing her hands, watching me mop up the oil in the cockpit and down the fuselage. Pat supplied some Varsol, and after about a half hour of work, IPL was looking a little more like her old self. We took off for Kingcome, only ten minutes' flying time from Sullivan, but encountered a violent thundershower

Telegraph Cove (near Port McNeill), as it was in the beginning: the sawmill supplied timber for local construction. The cove continues today as the whale-watching centre of the coast thanks to its proximity to Robson Bight, the orcas' chosen mating spot.

COLLEEN SINCLAIR PHOTO

84

completely localized to Kingcome Inlet. I figured I would give the frightened woman a break and go around the storm by taking an alternate route past the Scott Cove logging camp and into Kingcome via Bond Sound, all of which appeared to be in bright sunshine, with only a few black clouds overhead. As we proceeded to the logging camp, a bolt of lightning struck a promontory right abeam the aircraft, then one helluva clap of thunder burst right over us. I had never seen or heard anything like this, and the crash in my headphones just about blew my ears off. If you think it startled me, you should have heard Betty. She wanted out—*right now.*

"At Scott Cove," she said, voice quivering, pointing to the camp coming up over the nose. I couldn't talk her out of it. She was completely beside herself, so I landed at Scott Cove, and she hightailed it up the dock to the cookhouse, where I'm certain she regaled the staff with her story of the most terrifying flight anyone had ever endured, and with a replacement pilot to boot.

For my part, I flew back to Port Hardy and spent the rest of the day in the hangar, cleaning up the plane so that Beaver Bob wouldn't malign me for anything more than scaring the hell out of his cook.

When cleaning up the cockpit, I confirmed an earlier observation: the oil cap was not locking in place, and the slightest touch would unseat it. I flagged this malfunction by itemizing it in the journey logbook for the engineer to repair. Later, Beaver Bob took exception to this entry, explaining that the oil cap had always been like that and one simply had to take care that it wasn't dislodged. As I may have mentioned, Bob didn't smile much. He conveyed the impression that I was also responsible for the cloudburst and the lightning bolt.

Reaching the mandatory retirement age of 60 comes as a blow to a pilot in good health. After an adventurous life in the cockpit of bush planes, and then with the airlines, flying state-of-the-art airliners to far-flung destinations, blowing out the candles on one's 60th can be a choking experience. If you think this is a bad scene, consider Ken Sorko's story. I met Ken when I was the editor and publisher (and janitor) of Aviator *magazine.*

Cancel My Subscription

He didn't need a map, Ken Sorko. He could fly up Johnstone Strait at 50 feet with visibility down to a quarter mile, and make the turn into Clio Channel with ease. He did it every day, he and the Stranny. "The 90-mile-an-hour airplane," he called it: take off at 90, cruise at 90, land at 90.

Ken did not take kindly to rude comments passengers made about this venerable flying boat. So what that it was a biplane, with fabric-covered wings, lots of struts and wires, and two big old sleeve-valve radial engines.

"A throwback to pre-war," they would laugh.

"Yeah, the Crimean War," someone else would quip.

Ken's first landing would be at Minstrel Island to drop freight or passengers. The docks couldn't handle the big flying boat, because its wings would tangle with

Three wartime "Strannies" photographed near Ucluelet on the west coast of Vancouver Island. Designed for reconnaissance use, this old biplane carried depth charges for anti-submarine attacks. It could stay in the air for 12 hours flying at 90 miles per hour—its range was ... well, you can do the math.
RCAF PHOTO

all those pilings. So somebody would come out in a boat to get the passengers or the freight.

"You've got two going to town on the way back, Ken," would be the kind of airline bookings he got yelled at him as he cranked up the big engines to take off for the next stop.

Ken Sorko had something that was unique among aircraft flying the B.C. coast back in 1946. He had a two-way radio that gave him communication with Mrs. K at Alert Bay. He would get on the radio and tell her that they had one passenger out of Minstrel for the return trip. Mrs. K would give Ken the weather and the sea conditions at Alert Bay, as well as any passenger or

freight pick-ups on the books. Mrs. K was Edith Kenmore, who became a legend with coastal seaplane pilots and a particular hero to Ken.

"She knew the weather and she knew the sea," he explained. "She had a way with people that endeared her forever to the pilots."

The big Stranraer flying boats were introduced by Jim Spilsbury's Queen Charlotte Airlines following the Second World War and were credited with driving the steamships out of business along the B.C. coast. Four hours up the coast and four hours back was the duty day for a Stranny pilot like Ken Sorko. The stops were at logging camps, sport-fishing lodges and private float camps in the many waterways of the B.C. mid-coast in those days. Ken flew that route for a couple of years before taking all his bush-flying sense with him to Canadian Pacific Airlines, where he became a captain on a Douglas DC-6B four-engine airliner. He ultimately moved on to the big jets.

One could bet that Ken knew where he was at every moment while piloting these wonderful new airplanes on the exotic routes he now flew to Asia and the South Pacific. And I'm pretty sure that magnetic course, heading, drift and elapsed time were a constant commentary going on in Ken's mind while his young co-pilot fidgeted with punching

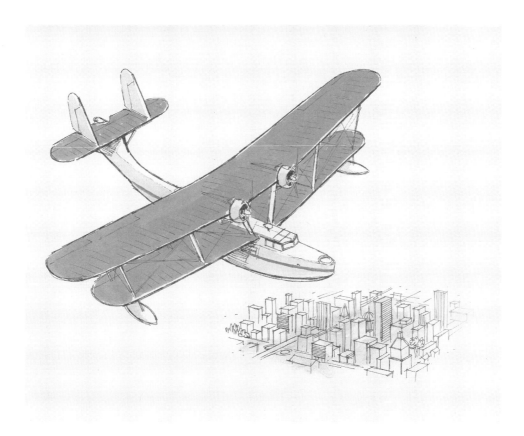

numbers into a black box—a black box that had never done a half-mile visibility approach over the dryback into Sullivan Bay in a 30-degree crosswind.

Ken contributed several stories to *Aviator* magazine during the early years of his retirement and was always a cheerleader for my publication. One day, following several months of not being in touch, he phoned me. His wife handled the dialling, and he came on the line when she made the connection.

"They tell me I've got Alzheimer's," Ken said. "I wanted to talk to you while I still had my marbles. Thanks for all the magazines and for telling all those great stories about the coastal pilots over the years. I can't read anymore, so I have to cancel my subscription. I just thought I'd call to say thanks."

I can't remember how I responded. Whatever I said was inadequate.

Not an unusual
"dock" for a seaplane.
Passengers had to
be nimble and very
quick when a log was
all that was available.

4

NOTAMs and Rivets

Things Mechanical

Joining the Dots

Since the stories related in this chapter have to do with some aspect of regulations governing the operation of aircraft in Canadian airspace, readers might benefit from a little inside skinny on air regs and those who enforce them.

There is a saying in the aviation industry: "When the paperwork weighs the same as the airplane, the craft is airworthy." The industry is totally governed by Transport Canada's Civil Aviation division, created by the Air Board in 1930, when it—belatedly—relieved the military of the job. This federal department operated originally as the DOT (Department of Transport), changed its name to MOT (Ministry of Transport) and now prevails under the simpler moniker of TC (Transport Canada). The other thing that changed over the years was that the original two-man B.C. regional office expanded into 12 storeys of office space on Vancouver's Burrard

ART COX

Street. This expansion occurred simultaneously with the exponential growth of air regulations, and some might infer that one was the cause of the other.

In 1938 Canada issued a published edition of the air regs. That was a 12-page scribbler. Today your airline pilot's large square flight bag—the one with the stickers all over it, with which he or she struggles to board the aircraft—is weighted only by a book of air regs and one day's change of underwear. It is a matter of record that pilots have one arm longer than the other, and it is no longer caused by swinging the props, but by hefting the book that governs their actions in the cockpit.

Learning to fly to private-pilot status now takes 45 hours of training rather than the 25 hours required in 1950. This increase is directly related to the complexity of operating under and understanding the plethora of regulations that keep airplanes from running into one another over Canada.

"NOTAM" is an abbreviation for notice to airmen. NOTAMs are issued by TC and advise about things that might affect one's flight, such as the military firing rockets at a certain time at a certain geographic location. These notices and the aircraft's journey logbook are the principal paperwork items pilots must pay attention to. Compared with AMEs (aircraft maintenance engineers), pilots have it easy. It is generally felt that engineers bear the brunt of the paper war, while pilots read NOTAMs and polish their sunglasses. The guy with all the wrenches in his back pocket spends hours each day maintaining records of work performed on aircraft, recording new parts and tagging old parts for quarantine storage, and maintaining a constant vigil for ADs (airworthiness directives). ADs require immediate action, such as grounding aircraft that have specific serial numbers and that have been manufactured with a doofinger formadoodle, which has developed a history of failing during tight turns close to the ground. SBs (service bulletins), by contrast, are of lower priority and merely suggest to the engineer that he might like to pull all Vultee Vibrators off the line in the next 100 hours because they seem to be developing loose wing bolts that should be tightened on the next 100-hour check.

Coastal pilots claim to get a nosebleed if they go over 800 feet, and flying off the water deep in the rainforest doesn't present much of a separation problem with other aircraft. You might think that air regs out in the bush would be no problem, but every so often the minions back in Ottawa get antsy about floatplanes. One can imagine them fuming: "Those macho, hairy bush pilots have got to toe the line."

On one occasion a missionary from Ottawa arrived at Port Hardy airport with a sheaf of papers, which he handed out to each of the pilots. On the page were a whole bunch of numbered dots, something like those little puzzles in which joining the dots results in a cartoon of some sort. But this was no cartoon; it was a "simplified" means of achieving a weight and balance calculation for a Beaver or an Otter. The empty weight of the airplane plus the weight of its gas and oil, passengers and freight are the obvious factors in calculating the aircraft's all-up weight, and loading the heavy stuff up forward as close to the centre of gravity as possible was standard practice. But coastal pilots hardly ever used the term "mean aerodynamic chord" when discharging Joe Logger with his six flats of Bud at Fanny Bay.

When informed that on a given route each aircraft might make 15 landings and take-offs, changing its weight and balance each time by dropping off and picking up a variety of passengers and freight, our man from head office was flummoxed. When asked where we were supposed to leave this form, he stated that it was to be left at our base at Port Hardy airport. He grew to realize that this would not be possible, because we were doing something of a milk run and wouldn't be back until just before grounding time. One bright apple suggested we carry a hammer and nails,

A Gulf Air Single Otter at the dock of M&B Logging in Kilbella Bay. Pilots worked harder when flying the Single Otter—freight loads of 2,000 pounds were regular fare.

and nail the completed form to a tree at each stop, because what good would it be aboard the airplane in the event of an accident?

There was a new stripper at the local pub that night, and the pilots took our man from Ottawa to the show. He displayed a decided leaning to Kokanee beer and laughingly admitted to being a leg man. We never saw him again. The papers with little numbered dots must have gone back with him, because they also disappeared.

This is not to be understood as a putdown of the aviation authorities, who perform a vital and essential job. Rather, it is to point out that throughout the short history of flying, floatplanes have had a hard time conforming to many regulations that had land-based airliners in mind when they were drafted. In the days of the stories in this book, the "three-rivet Plimsoll line" was in general use. Pilots, loading the aircraft based on their own experience, would not exceed a load that brought the water line up to the bottom of the third rivet down from the float deck at the rear of the pontoon. It doesn't take a visit to the local strip club to know that this system is hard to beat.

ART COX

Willa, Eleanor, Olive, Helen, Anne, Cheryl and Colleen are the names of some of the women in my life. DST, CHR, XRK, OQU, RQW and JOM are the names of some of the airplanes in my life. I did not have to look in my diaries to recall the names of those ladies, nor did I have to check my logbooks to remember the planes—one never forgets a lover.

Move the "F" Over

While none of the aforementioned women will be too enamoured with the comparison, pilots will all agree that the name of an aircraft—its assigned registered identity, its three-letter "ident"—lives on in the mind and becomes related to specific events in one's flying life. A pilot will start his hangar-flying story something like this: "I was flying JOM, a beautiful Beaver, on the day I met this gorgeous woman. She sat in the co-pilot seat with a little boy on her lap. She asked me if I would accept a cheque in payment for the flight. I accepted the cheque, and damned if I didn't end up marrying this woman! The cheque cleared and the marriage … well, it hasn't bounced yet." (I had to tell that one because she's going to ask me about those other names.)

Back in the days when Canada was linked to Britain by more than a beaver

When Transport Canada ordered owners to "Move the 'F' Over," CF-OQU became C-FOQU. One wag commented that the phonetic pronunciation reflected the pilot's attitude.

pelt tribute, our aircraft bore British registrations—GC was the national identifier that the king or queen of England hung on early Canadian aircraft. The G was followed by a dash, then the C and an additional three letters such as ART. All that resulted in G-CART being painted 30 inches high on the side of the plane and on the underside of the wing. You didn't want to have a short fuselage back in those days, or you'd never get it all on.

When Canada set up its own registration system, the national designator became CF, followed by a dash and the three letters, such as ART, resulting in CF-ART. That system prevailed until 1970, when the number of aircraft in Canada had increased to the point that a four-letter ident was required. Those of us who had aircraft bearing the old CF designation were told to move the F over. Not a rude request, as it turned

out, because the dash became the middle bar of the F, and the new dash separating the C from the four letters (are you still with me?) was created from the centre bar of the old F (you're lost, methinks). Our example aircraft now became C-FART (whoops!).

The reason I chose ART at the outset was to show that problems could arise when using four letters. The civil aviation authorities were very clever, though, and seemingly never issued an ident that would prove to be a phonetic embarrassment. My aircraft at the time was OQU and it became FOQU—which, I suppose, was as close to a phonetic joke as it got.

Once all the existing aircraft had made this change, a provision for newly registered aircraft was established: instead of an F, new registrations were assigned a G. So it was now possible for two aircraft to have the same three-letter ident, but one would be prefaced by an F, the other by a G. This changeover of registrations led to a period in Canadian aviation history known as the "Are you a Foxtrot or a Golf?" era, in which control towers repeated that question whenever pilots transmitted only the last three letters of their ident. For readers unfamiliar with the international phonetic alphabet used in radio transmissions, Foxtrot and Golf are the accepted phonetics for F and G. So one became a Foxtrot or a Golf—and this system, you will understand, was developed to make everything very clear and understandable.

Only once did I fly into a control zone with another aircraft having the same ident as mine—he was the G, and I was the F, and both of us failed to mention this. I'm sure the controller would have enjoyed reminding us to move the F over, but this time he would have meant it quite another way.

The Small World of Airplanes

The significance of an aircraft's identifying letters was brought home to me in a sad way on a dock at Towry Head, at the top end of Loughborough Inlet. I had just tied up behind a Cessna 180 with the ident C-FZSZ. I knew both the plane and the pilot, Ed Carder. What I didn't know was what John Uzell, the Towry Head logging contractor, was going to tell me when I joined him on the ramp. John had been standing there for several minutes when I walked along the dock toward him. He seemed transfixed and didn't take his eyes off the little orange and white Cessna.

"That's my dad's plane," he said as I mounted the ramp. I was confused and was about to explain that it belonged to Ed Carder of Minstrel Air when John added, "At least, it was my dad's

plane—ZSZ—for many years: he was killed in it."

"John, I didn't realize that," was my limp response.

"He was attempting to let down through scud at our camp. Stalled into the water from a tight turn in fog—six years ago, now. The plane was rebuilt, and here it is on my dock. Shit!" He walked past me and under the wing of ZSZ to his own Cessna 180, parked in front of what must have been the worst of his memories. He tailed off his aircraft and, with a final look back, swung into the pilot seat and taxied away.

A year later, in 1981, ZSZ claimed its second victim when it and pilot Ed Carder disappeared for all time somewhere between Kingcome Village and the head of Knight Inlet. Twenty-five years after that, John Uzell, piloting his Beaver with four of his workmen aboard, stalled out of a tight turn while manoeuvring in low visibility. The aircraft carried John and his passengers to their deaths in precisely the same manner as John's father had perished—plunging into the forest behind the company logging camp.

CSI: Crash Scene Investigation

When the Transportation Safety Board (TSB) dismantled the GPS device on board John Uzell's crashed Beaver, they were able to reconstruct the action

Pictured on the dock at Alert Bay, Beaver RQW was a long-serving coastal seaplane that became Orca Air's first aircraft in 1982. The AirBC logo remained on the plane until the official transfer of the licences had taken place.

of the aircraft's last moments: it had penetrated fog in an attempt to reach the camp, then aborted the action by performing a steep banking turn, presumably back to an area of better visibility. It then cruised back and forth for a few moments (presumably looking for a hole in the scud) and repeated the attempt. This time, the banking manoeuvre to exit the danger area was too steep for the aircraft's load. The up-going wing stalled, causing the aircraft to roll onto its back and plunge, nose down, into the trees.

This analysis by the TSB revealed a further disturbing fact: the pilot manual for all de Havilland Beavers did not contain any explanation of the stall characteristics associated with a common chord wing such as the

type used on this aircraft. The testing requirements in effect in 1947, when the Beaver first flew, required neither a test nor notations describing such a stall. This meant that a succession of pilots over the years, being checked out on the Beaver, were never officially informed of this characteristic. Most pilots would agree that they could determine that the stall tendency applied to such a wing design without its being noted in the pilot manual, but this is a broad assumption, and check pilots need to draw the attention of new pilots to the problem.

Unfortunately, no one will "officially" alter the Beaver pilot manual to include this information, lest they be held liable for the information not being there in the first place.

The chief engineer of an airline will often be seen conferring with the operations manager. They will both be referring to a slip of paper torn from an old envelope and bearing a scrawled number—a number like 32.4—and somewhere else on that scrap an aircraft ident—let's say, FHT. This homely piece of paper could be called a TBO (time before overhaul) notification. Airplanes and the parts that make them run, things like propellers, engines, magnetos, generators and alternators, each have a TBO.

The chief engineer has a blackboard that is lined off and shows each aircraft in the fleet. Also shown is the TBO for each plane, indicated as the number of flying hours at which it must come in for inspection. In this scenario, the engineer is giving the operations manager advance notice that FHT has 32.4 hours of flying time left before being taken off the flight line for scheduled maintenance. By studying that aircraft's technical log, the engineer will know that certain accessories will also expire by then, and replacement parts must be ready or on order from the suppliers. With these accessories will come a variety of tags and documents attesting to the overhaul work performed by the Transport Canada-approved overhaul shop. These items, along with the engineer's installation remarks, will be stapled into the tech log to attest that the required work was done and that authentic replacement parts were used.

TBO

When I last flew FHT, it had totalled 32,000 flying hours on the airframe, and I recently heard that it is up to 37,000 hours. This aircraft, number 50 off the 1947 de Havilland Beaver assembly line, must have a lot of old technical logbooks, each bulging with the tags and documents that have been attached over the years during many inspections.

When the Transport Canada airworthiness inspector strolls into the hangar, he or she is concerned about this information and the systems employed to quarantine expired parts so that they don't find their way back into an airplane by mistake.

ART COX

98

Aircraft maintenance engineers are as dedicated to the industry as pilots are, and a professionally operated airline, no matter how small, will not attempt to short-circuit this basic and vital safety system. But it can happen, inadvertently, if somebody isn't riding the system and keenly disposed to keeping track of things. Small operators and private owners working in the bush are particularly vulnerable. They usually have a maintenance contract with the closest service depot, which nevertheless can be hundreds of miles away. Without a mechanic close at hand, the problems can compound. Here's a case in point.

I found the Beaver ready to go in the hangar of a maintenance operator at La Ronge, Saskatchewan, on May 12, 1989. The plane displayed the registration C-FMAS, which meant it had once belonged to the Manitoba Government Air Services. It had been sold by that owner and totally rebuilt by Al Beaulieu in Vancouver, before finding its home here at a fishing lodge on Kasba Lake, 400 miles north of La Ronge and just a tad north of 60 degrees latitude. Beaulieu had installed all the Kenmore modifications, and it was a very comfortable Beaver to fly. It was needed at the fishing resort 400 miles north, where I would be flying it and ferrying the lodge's customers for the next three months. At that time, Kasba Lake Lodge had its own 4,000-foot dirt strip for use by Canadian Airlines, who brought our guests and those of a nearby lodge into the strip in a Fokker 27, a 60-passenger commuter aircraft.

The other lodge had its own Single Otter floatplane that would normally haul passengers from Kasba to the other lodge's resort on Obre Lake, but often the Otter was so busy that MAS would be contracted to do the work. Such was the case one rainy day quite late into the three-month season. I had been flying steadily for a couple of months, logging many hours on the aircraft, and MAS had performed without a problem. This was good, because "problem" in this country would be spelled in capital letters—the land is a barren wilderness.

On this drizzly day, the Obre Lake passengers came down to the seaplane dock still wearing their city street clothes and acting understandably stunned as they tried to comprehend the sudden change from civilization to subarctic tundra, and perhaps they were even wondering why they were here. There were five of them, with gear, and as we taxied out onto the lake for take-off, their combined breathing fogged up the windows. The smell of their damp headgear and topcoats was less than appealing. I was chirping away trying to make things brighter as I explained where the life jackets were located—always a topic that cheers people up when they're taking their first flight in a 60-year-old plane.

We took off into the now driving rain, heading to Obre Lake. As we levelled off at 1,000 feet, I turned around to tell the happy group that the trip would be only about eight minutes and that the lodge had the soup pot on high. Suddenly, *bang*—a helluva backfire from the engine. I had never had a backfire from a 985 before. It startled me, and of course the five passengers were ecstatic. I was closer to home than to our destination, so I turned back, checking all the gauges and trying to figure out what had caused that explosion in the exhaust system—if that's what it was. We began our descent for the lodge and were down to about 600 feet turning final, when all went quiet up front—just the prop windmilling. We deadsticked onto the water and came off the step about 50 feet from the dock. Of course, the lodge people were surprised to see us back so soon and wondered what the hell I was doing with that paddle.

Later, when everyone had gone up

The author's son, Peter, filling up the old man's airplane at Port McNeill, about 1983. Orca Air operated a popular scheduled service from Port McNeill to all the communities on the adjacent mainland. The sched service operated on an "as the traffic warrants" basis, which often resulted in six flights a day.

to the dining room, Harold, the camp manager, and I found the cause of the backfire and engine failure. It turned out to be both magnetos. The first mag had failed with the backfire, and the second one just died on final for the landing. "Horseshoes up your ass," Harold observed.

Both magnetos had been installed new on the same date. That model of Bendix magneto has a 1,000-hour TBO, and unbeknownst to me, we had reached that 1,000 hours. The first mag quit right on the money, and the second one gave us about ten minutes longer. I found this hard to believe, but

it was confirmed by the engineer when he reluctantly came up from La Ronge several days later to make the repair.

Transport Canada requires that an airline appoint a maintenance coordinator—not necessarily an engineer—to keep track of these things by maintaining a watch over the aircraft's journey logbook and the tech log. Nobody was doing that, and the magnetos died in flight, right on schedule.

To this day, the Obre Lake experience is one that comes to mind when I'm awake in the dead of night and a vagrant thought brings to mind a question starting with "What if ... "

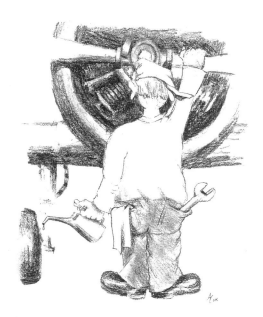

ART COX

Back in 1990, when I first began publishing BC Aviator magazine, it was deemed a good business move to align the publication with one of the many associations in this industry. There were no pilots' associations, except for the pilots' trade unions, so the magazine fell in with aircraft engineers, who belong to a Canada-wide organization that represents the trade's position on aircraft maintenance issues with Transport Canada. I was suddenly made aware that engineers play a more vital role in the aviation industry than pilots do. Decisions made on the hangar floor, not in the cockpit, have long been the force that shapes the aviation industry.

Nuts and Bolts

For years, aircraft maintenance engineers (AMEs) were called mechanics. This was truly a misnomer, because anyone planning to work on airplanes had quite a few academic training hoops to jump through, plus much required practical experience, before being allowed to turn a wrench on even a lowly Piper Cub. One might associate the word "mechanic" with a guy in coveralls who has a mechanical bent for dropping and chopping your average Ford Model A, but airplanes require a shade more training, understanding and responsibility.

For many years, the licensing of engineers was specialized—a licence for propeller work, another for structural and sheet metal, another for engine work and so on, plus an endorsement system for approval on specific aircraft types. A few years ago, Transport Canada's airworthiness department revised the licensing

The nose wheels on an amphibious Beaver retract upward and lie over onto the pontoon deck. These wheels, when retracted, are fully visible to the pilot. The main gear retracts inside the pontoon at the step compartment. The amphibious gear is a high-maintenance item that adds considerable cost to the plane's operation.

102

requirements and did away with some of the specialty certificates. Long-time engineers were some choked at what they saw as a move to marginalize their lifelong achievements in the industry. They grumbled that the major airlines favoured the one-licence-fits-all concept so that the companies could hire just one engineer, who would then sign off on the work of some high school dropout employed to perform the job. This was, of course, a rancorous view of the change, but when the smoke cleared, it was hard to know who benefited from the new licensing process. That sardonic "mechanic" cum AME, armed with an open-end wrench, is apt to attribute the whole process to the need for TC minions in Ottawa to fill their pre-retirement years

with a sense of purpose, but the reality is that Canadian airplanes, hewing to TC standards, are well maintained in the face of fast-changing technologies, and the AMEs who perform the work are as good as any in the world. Having said that, I'll bet that the paperwork increased and came closer to the all-up weight of the aircraft when the new licensing system was established.

In aircraft engineering as well as piloting, there is a potential hazard referred to as the "human factor." AMEs have been addressing this fly in the ointment for some years now, and procedures have been developed in aircraft maintenance to ensure that human errors don't occur—errors like the one that created the "Hawaiian Convertible," the Aloha Airlines 737

A pilot's worst enemy is glassy water; landing on a mirror requires strict attention to an instrument-type controlled landing procedure. Over the years, this sunny-day hazard has been the cause of many mishaps and lives lost—all correctly attributed to pilot error.

that shed its skin in flight in 1988 and left the stunned passengers riding a virtual open platform in the sky. The luckless flight attendant was the only person not tied down, and she paid with her life when the upper half of the fuselage was swept into the slipstream. Miraculously, the flight crew landed the abbreviated Boeing without any further loss of life.

What does this have to do with the "human factor"? Well, the plane had just been returned to the flight line by Aloha's maintenance department, having undergone an extensive check of every single rivet on the fuselage. This check is required after a certain number of flying hours, a number that airplane had reached. Men were suspended by ropes from the hangar ceiling so that they could walk the topside of the fuselage—the part that came unglued—seeking evidence of hairline cracks in the skin at each rivet. They gave the aircraft a clean bill of health. When the remains of the plane were re-examined after the accident, there was evidence of a multitude of hairline cracks at all the rivet locations. How, then, did it get signed out as airworthy? Studies attributed psychological considerations—"human factor" reasons—rather than unprofessional workmanship or indifference, and the accident has since been used in training procedures as an outstanding example of not seeing and identifying what is there in front of your eyes.

On the flying side of the industry, a 2007 flying disaster in Brazil might also be attributed to the human factor. Why did the pilot elect to land—and why was he cleared to land—on a notoriously short runway in a heavy rainstorm without first obtaining a James Brake figure, which measures the likelihood of hydroplaning? He determined after touchdown that he wasn't going to make good the landing and attempted to power back into the air, but he didn't make it; nor did 176 passengers and 15 people on the ground. Perhaps the James Brake information was not available at this Brazilian airport, which already had a history of safety concerns.

There is an international aviation advocacy organization that demands worldwide compliance to safety standards, but it would seem that this Brazilian airport's problem slipped through the cracks. While we can breathe easy in Canada with respect to safety requirements, that might not be the story in countries of lesser political stability, eh?

5

MEMORIES THAT GO CLUNK IN THE NIGHT

Scary Stuff

Worst Fears Realized

To this day, the thought of them puts my stomach in a knot, and I quickly think of something else. Every pilot who has ever flown in the bush has got at least one event that he would rather not recall. I have three. If something triggers a recollection of any of these events, I'm apt to call out: "I want my crayons!"

I asked five coastal pilots to contribute their worst nightmare story to this chapter, and they all said they didn't have one. This would suggest that their superior piloting skills prevented anything untoward from occurring while they were holding down the pilot seat. Each of these guys was also very handsome and very rich, drove E-type Jags and had a Hollywood starlet for a mistress. So you get only this author's nightmares, because his Jaguar is in for maintenance and Charlize Theron has found a younger man.

My three nightmare stories are "Chicken Little and the Giant Hand," "For Whom the Bell Cranks" and "Seven Come Eleven." The last event is the worst one. I don't even want to go into many details—it was a case of *what could have been* rather than what was, and I never followed up on the event to determine the consequences, if any, for the other guy. There was proof that it was not I who'd erred, which was a relief, and I succeeded in driving the "what if" thought from my mind until now. If there are spelling mistakes in this anecdote, they were caused by my now sweaty palms which made my fingers slip on the keys.

The "TBO" story in the previous chapter doesn't give me the willies, so it doesn't qualify as a bad dream—but it should. Instead, my reaction has been incredulity: how can two components fail simultaneously and at the precise number of hours of operation permitted by the components' assigned "time before overhaul"? Sufficient to say that a sense of wonder precludes the stomach qualms in that *Fate Is the Hunter* type of adventure.

"For Whom the Bell Cranks" is sort of a proof that when your number's up, your number's up. I'm not suggesting that this was part of poet John Donne's message back in the 17th century, when he, not Hemingway or Gary Cooper or

Ingrid Bergman, penned that sobering bell toll. I apologize for the contrived title—it was just irresistible.

The "Giant Hand" experience could easily be interpreted as a religious event if you're inclined to apply mystical explanations to natural phenomena. At the moment that these frightening events take place, there is a tendency toward "foxhole religion," as it was called in the Second World War. But a meteorologist can set you straight with terms like adiabatic winds, pressure gradients, Venturi effect and the like. So you don't have to wear a funny hat like the pope's and wonder how to wear your headphones too.

*A pilot friend of mine was taking off from the top end of Rivers Inlet when
a Giant Hand picked up the Grumman Goose and slammed it down on
the water with such force that the wing, with both engines attached, was
peeled back like the top of a sardine can. In this startling event, one of the
passenger-sardines was pitched out of the plane and into the water, and
was saved from drowning only by the fast action of the pilot. The other
passengers were literally and figuratively shaken up, suffering what
the press is apt to call non-life-threatening injuries. The aircraft,
which now resembled a big canoe, was a write-off. When the pilot
wrote his accident report, he would be hard pressed to describe what
actually happened to cause the wreck. Reference to the "Giant Hand"
wouldn't cut it, but I have had similar experiences on two occasions, and
it's the best description for this most frightening of phenomena.*

Chicken Little and the Giant Hand

Boswell Inlet runs adjacent to and sort of parallel with Rivers Inlet. Coastal pilots
fly between these two major waterways through a little channel known as Draney.
Outflowing winds also whistle through Draney, picking up speed from the Venturi
effect of this constricted passage. There is a logging camp in a little bay in Boswell
Inlet adjacent to Draney, and that camp is a regular stop for the daily sched flight.

On a lovely September afternoon, I landed an amphibious Beaver straight into
the bay, coming off the step just at the entrance so that my landing wake wouldn't
rattle the boats tied up at the camp dock. My docking was uneventful, and my
single passenger jumped out as I started to tie up the plane. He grabbed the wing
rope and held the plane against the dock as I knelt to tie off the rear strut painter.

As I knelt there on the dock, a blast of wind came through Boswell, making a

This fuel stop at the mouth of Rivers Inlet was the home of "Lucky" Bachan, who'd been a tail gunner in a Lancaster bomber during the Second World War. Bachan survived a record 36 missions over Germany, and many years after the war he was invited to attend an international fighter pilots' reunion. There, former Luftwaffe pilots who had once fired at him now bought him drinks.

90-degree turn into the bay. It picked up a 45-gallon oil drum full of rainwater and threw it 50 feet, into the side of a tin warehouse building. The Beaver took the wind under the right wing and heeled over against the dock at such an angle that I thought the left wingtip was going to touch the dock. Both the passenger and I threw ourselves onto the dock and hung on to the tie-up rail for fear of being blown into the water.

As quickly as the wind had appeared, it stopped and all was calm again. Both of us were amazed at the suddenness and the power of the gust and its sudden disappearance. We tied up the plane and walked up to the camp, which was on a knoll overlooking the bay. No one at the cookhouse had felt the wind, and after listening to our story, they thought we had been smoking something. I had a coffee with the superintendent before returning to the plane and taxiing out for take-off to

return to Port Hardy. At the mouth of the bay, the water was a little choppy and a brisk breeze was outflowing from Boswell Inlet, so I turned into wind, pointed the plane into the inlet and commenced my take-off run.

The Beaver had travelled no more than 100 feet when suddenly it lifted off the water in a fairly high-nose attitude and developed a hellish rate of climb—1,200 feet per minute, in a plane that normally wouldn't give you more than 300 feet per minute. I stuffed the nose down and throttled back from take-off power. The attitude changed, but the VSI (vertical speed indicator) still indicated 1,200 feet per minute. I was now holding a nose-down attitude and had decreased power, but I was still going up like a rocket. The mountain beside me topped at 1,200 feet, and when I reached that altitude, the updraft quit and I started down at the same hellish rate of descent. I laid on full take-off power and held the nose slightly high. The Beaver "arrived" onto the water as a helicopter would land—with seemingly no forward speed. To my amazement it was a soft landing, but I had no time for congratulatory sighs of relief. The outflow was now blasting out of the inlet, making a turn downwind impossible, and I wasn't going to try another take-off into that maelstrom.

I left the water rudders up, dropped flap and throttled back to idle, allowing the wind to carry the aircraft back down the inlet to the point where I could again enter the bay at the logging camp. This worked, but it required me to steer the tail around by opening the pilot doors alternately on either side of the plane. It took me 45 minutes to sail the plane backward to the mouth of the bay. When I got back to the dock, the superintendent was surprised to see me. He had heard my take-off, performed out of sight of the camp, and figured that I was long gone to Port Hardy.

The wind continued to howl at an awesome speed down the inlet, so, being chicken-hearted, I planned to spend the night at the camp. Considering the power of that wind, I was concerned about the safety of the plane. The camp mechanic helped me hang a 20-gallon pail of water from the outboard ring of the lift strut and wrap a rope around that wing to spoil the airfoil.

I spent the night at the camp and returned to Port Hardy the next morning. My story was disbelieved by all, and I think I won the silent accolade as Wimp of the Month. This happened long before the Grumman was trashed by a similar force, so maybe today those doubters would believe that the Giant Hand giveth and the Giant Hand taketh away.

My second Giant Hand experience took place in somewhat the same area, only farther north, where Fisher Channel opens into Fitz Hugh Sound. I arrived there in a Beaver amphib with two passengers aboard. We had departed Bella Coola with full tanks and the firm belief that it was a beautiful day for flying airplanes. This consideration was substantiated by a weather report provided to us by the new, privately operated meteorological station at Bella Coola airport. The federal environment ministry had, at that time, decided to decommission lighthouses and privatize meteorological stations—remote TV cameras and telemetering were the new employees, replacing the living, breathing lighthouse keepers. The telemetering figures from a remote anemometer at the mouth of Fisher Channel indicated a southeast wind of four knots—or so the new civilian meteorological officer advised. Hey, we were fat and happy as we trucked down Fisher into Fitz Hugh.

Wham! The wind that slammed into the slab-sided Beaver as we emerged into Fitz Hugh Sound was no four knots—it was as if we had flown into a high-pressure fire hose—and not only did we weathercock into wind with no control input from me, but with no change in level flight attitude, we went into a rapid descent. We had been flying at 800 feet, but were down to 400 feet above a raging sea before I could check the descent with take-off power. My adrenalin surged as the passenger beside me, startled by the impact of the wind and the sudden change in our environment, pulled out a set of beads and commenced mouthing some Hail Marys.

Although I had stopped the descent, I couldn't climb the aircraft because any attempt to pull the nose up bled off the airspeed required to maintain level flight. Any reduction in power would bring us down to the water. There is a limit to how long you can hold take-off boost, and I was frantically looking for answers. I cranked in ten degrees of flap, despite the airspeed being above flap speed, and got a 50-foot-per-minute climb rate at take-off power. This Beaver was equipped with loran, a new technology at that time which, among other things, gave a readout of speed over the ground in knots. It was indicating 22 knots over the water with an airspeed of 106 knots, which meant I had an 84-knot headwind that was somehow exerting its force downward on the Beaver (the Giant Hand effect).

I quickly figured out that this downward force was caused by the coastal topography, so despite the godawful look of things out to sea, I directed the aircraft on a course that would put me well out to sea on the west side of Calvert Island—a fearful place to be in these conditions, but a turn downwind was out of the question. It worked. Gradually, I regained the ability to climb and was able to distance the Beaver from that raging ocean. At the same time, my ground speed increased to 26 knots—that's only 26 nautical miles travelled every hour, and I was burning 20 gallons per hour. I was glad I had started with full tanks.

My passenger was still frantically fingering his beads, and my response wasn't a whole lot more rational: transmitting too many position reports to the base dispatcher, who I later learned was the second-most-frightened person in this whole escapade. It ended well, though: the wind subsided as we neared Port Hardy airport.

I suspect that my earlier title, Wimp of the Month, gave way to the new, more enduring one: Chicken Little.

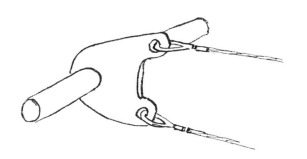

The chance of a mechanical failure is always a pilot's worst nightmare. The thought of a loss of power while over the ocean or over a mountain peak provides the incentive for pilots to check and recheck their machine's vital signs. Amazingly, those well-designed 1927 engines, when regularly and fastidiously maintained, are highly reliable. The chief concern for pilots is that rare occasion when an engineer develops "finger trouble." Here are a couple of stories in which an engineer's DNA could be found at the scene of the accident.

For Whom the Bell Cranks

They are shaped like a boomerang, in the form of an equilateral triangle. They are employed throughout aircraft engine and flight control systems, and are known as bell cranks. I don't know where the name came from; although it's a colourful moniker, it doesn't really tell you what bell cranks do, except maybe the "crank" part of it. Perhaps someone by the name of Bell invented them. Bell cranks are used to transfer energy or motion from one direction to the opposite direction. For instance, advancing the throttle in a Cessna 185 means that you are pushing a rod (significantly, it is called a push-rod) attached to one ear of a bell crank. Attached to the other ear is another push-rod that carries the now reversed motion toward the engine firewall, where it connects to a fuel pump. The fuel pump is opened and closed by this rod in gradations, depending on whether you are pouring on the

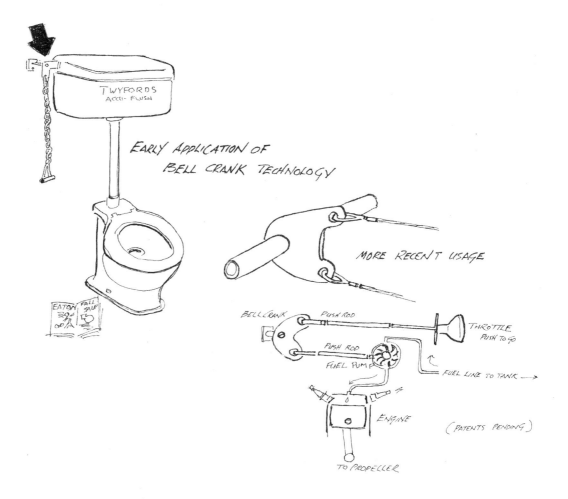

EARLY APPLICATION OF
BELL CRANK TECHNOLOGY

TWYFORDS
ACCU-FLUSH

MORE RECENT USAGE

BELL CRANK   PUSH ROD   THROTTLE
PUSH TO GO

PUSH ROD
FUEL PUMP

FUEL LINE TO TANK →

ENGINE

(PATENTS PENDING)

TO PROPELLER

coal or throttling back. Ingenious, but there's nothing new about bell cranks: they have been employed in similar fashion since the Industrial Revolution, so if there was a Mr. Bell who invented them, he must have had mutton chops and worn a top hat.

If you care to stay aboard that 185 and crawl down what engineers call the "tunnel"—down the tapering fuselage toward the tail—you will get tangled up in the elevator control wires, which are attached to—you guessed it—a bell crank. The top wire is put in play

Qualicum airport as it is today. The author, once a resident of Qualicum and a member of the local flying club, helped create this airport from a pasture donated by the Kinsmen Club. Neither the city fathers nor the provincial government would entertain the cost of paving the strip until Her Majesty, Queen Elizabeth II, decided to fly in to visit a friend. Suddenly the gravel strip, including taxiways, was paved, and a lovely terminal building was built in record time. The Queen must have been impressed, as are today's visiting pilots.

when you pull the control column back to make the aircraft climb, while the bottom cable, attached to the lower ear of the bell crank, is doing the work when you stuff the plane's nose down. While you are down there, you might observe what this device is made of and how it attaches to the "torque tube" of the elevator.

I hope I'm not blinding you with science. To make it all abundantly clear, the drawing at the beginning of this story, though something of a spoof, shows a bell crank attached to an elevator torque tube. Let me interject that we are definitely going somewhere with all this technical stuff. The elevator bell crank is made of cast aluminum. The holes to which the cables are attached are bushed with a stainless steel insert, and the clevis pin, also made of steel, is fused to the control cable. Cast aluminum, when immersed in salt water, dissolves only a little more slowly than a sugar lump in your coffee, so if you fly seaplanes on the B.C. coast, you or your appointed engineer should keep an eye on elevator bell cranks.

And this is where we are going with all this information—a simple little story that wakes me up some nights.

I had been flying all week out of Port Hardy airport and was driving down-island to my home at Qualicum Beach. Passing through the outskirts of Campbell River, I decided to visit some old stomping grounds and turned in at the Freshwater Marina seaplane base. I could expect to see some old buddies there. The only person on the seaplane tarmac was a logging contractor who owned a Cessna 180, against which he was leaning with a disconsolate look on his face. His face brightened when he saw me.

"Hey, just the guy I need to talk to," he said. "How would you like to earn 100 bucks for an hour's work?"

I was not too eager at the outset of this conversation—my logger friend had a checkered flying reputation, and I needed details before responding.

"I was just about to fly the groceries into camp when I got an emergency call for a breakdown part for one of our spar trees. If you could fly the groceries into the cookhouse, I could head down to Madill's in Nanaimo to pick up the part. It's just a 20-minute flight for you into my camp."

The logger's 180 was piled high with the camp groceries, and the plane had already been picked up onto the

float dolly and was ready for launching down the ramp into the river. I was familiar with the camp, and it was a beautiful day to fly, so I agreed. He was ecstatic.

"Here's your 100 bucks." He peeled off five 20-dollar bills. "The key's in the ignition. Just run her up the ramp when you get back. Hutch here will pick you up," he said, gesturing to the seaplane dock manager, who had now joined us beside the plane. With that, my logger friend jumped into his car and sped out of the marina. I climbed into his plane and started the engine as Hutch trucked me down the ramp and into the river.

As I taxied down the river, I checked over the panel, the seat adjustment and the general "feel" of this airplane. I would fly this one carefully until I got to know just how heavy a load had been put aboard and how she trimmed out in flight. Other than that, a Cessna 180 is a Cessna 180.

Take-offs out of Campbell River are performed at the river mouth, and one has to negotiate several gravel bars in this arm of the river. I was glad I knew from years of local flying where they were located, because the bars didn't show in the prevailing tide and could easily snag a seaplane for a long, embarrassing period while it waited to be freed by a higher tide.

Gulf Air's dock at the Campbell River Spit: Two airlines vied for the business out of Campbell River— Gulf Air and Island Airlines. Though competitors, they conducted themselves amicably and often helped each other out of tight situations. When AirBC took over, they joined forces under one flag.

The mag check was good; oil and cylinder head temperatures were in the green, and cycling the prop proved that the pitch control system was working okay. We arrived at the river mouth, and as an AirBC Beaver cleared into the Campbell River Spit, I retracted the water rudders and laid on full power for the take-off. During those first few seconds of full power, I cycled the ailerons—full deflection each way determined that they were correctly rigged—and applied full-up elevator. The elevator went up, then fell down—*bang!* I powered off and craned around to see the elevator hanging in the full-down position while I held the control column full back.

Little goosebumps rose on the back of my neck. I taxied back up the river, ramped the airplane and left the 100 bucks and the ignition key with Hutch, advising him of the problem and emphasizing that nobody should be allowed to fly that airplane. I drove home and had a great weekend, pushing aside the icy hand in the gut that told me I had missed buying the farm by about 30 seconds. That was my introduction to Mr. Bell's invention and the saltwater corrosion of Cessna bell cranks.

If you are like me, you will probably not find that near miss very exciting. After all, I did the control check that revealed the defect, and the result was then very predictable. If I hadn't done the control check, the full-powered dive into the water after take-off would be attributed to pilot error, and it would be a much more exciting tale. But there would be no one around to tell it.

So, if that's a ho-hum yarn, try another bell crank story:

There I was, with everything on the

clock as it should be, in a Cessna 185, tooling along at 1,200 feet above pristine mountain inlets. The sun through the Plexiglas was warm and comforting. I was what pilots call "fat and stupid": fat, meaning lots of fuel, and stupid—well, let's say that steely look on my face was a practised condition and in truth, the film was off the cogs. Suddenly, all the needles went to zero. This was followed by a sudden silence. Some would argue that the silence came first, but I was looking at the needles and they beat the silence by a nanosecond. I was flying over a 1,000-foot hill on the south side of Chancellor Channel, and if I didn't do something quick, I would be wearing the trees. I performed a 180-degree descending turn down the mountainside, trading height for airspeed, and alighted (don't you like that word?) on the glassy waters of the channel, close enough to the shore that my momentum would have carried me gently to the beach. But, instead, I dropped the water rudders and turned away from the safety of the beach. I had suddenly realized that the engine was running; it was ticking over at about 300 rpm. I advanced the throttle but nothing happened—the prop just ticked over, carrying the plane forward at about three nautical miles per hour.

At the other end of the channel there was a logging camp, so I pointed the plane toward it and "ticked" my way along for exactly one hour before arriving close enough to spot two men working on the camp's dock. They were very surprised to see me, having witnessed my landing up the channel and not realized I was in trouble. They were building the dock and ramp for a new logging operation that hadn't moved in yet, so I joined them in their powerboat to travel to nearby Kelsey Bay, where they were staying. Before leaving the aircraft, I removed the top cowling and cast my jaundiced eye over the engine. There it was, glaring at me: the throttle bell crank, hanging loose on the end of the throttle push-rod. How did it get that way?

The industry calls it the "human factor" in aviation. As I buttoned on the cowling, I called it the less delicate but more accurate name of "that god-damned engineer" who had so recently installed the engine on this plane. He had failed to use rod-ends on the ends of the push-rods, and the motor's vibration had worried the attachment bolt through the bell crank to freedom. This had been my third deadstick landing resulting from this guy's inept work, and I was ticked off.

What's a rod-end? Forget it: we pilots wear sunglasses and have exciting sex lives.

There was a story that did a circuit around Vancouver airport; it might have been fabricated, but I like to think it was true. Radio procedures are well established and adhered to by professional pilots and controllers, clarity and brevity being the keynotes of transmissions. On this day, an aircraft requested a time check from the tower. Since the aircraft had failed to identify itself, the controller came back with this: "If you are Air Canada, the local time is 15:45. If you are WestJet, it is a quarter to four. If you are the flying club, the little hand is almost on the four and the big hand is on the nine."

Use of the international phonetic alphabet becomes second nature to aviators, and when I'm stalled in traffic I sometimes find myself translating the licence plate of the car ahead of me into phonetics. If you have ever wondered why the phonetic alphabet is used in aircraft radio transmissions, the following story will clear that up.

Seven Come Eleven

For a three-month period one summer, I was flying a little twin-engined airplane back and forth between a large, busy international airport and a small resort town's paved strip. There were seven return flights a day on this short haul, and I swear the airplane soon knew its own way. The little airline for which I was flying had what is referred to as a "canned" flight plan filed with the international airport's tower, from which information the controllers knew that at about one-hour intervals this little 12-place twin would be arriving or departing. The airline was assigned an identifying number, in this case eleven, and the first flight into the busy international airport each morning was eleven-oh-seven (1107): eleven as the airline ident and seven (assigned by the airline) as my first morning flight number, to correspond with my time of departure from the resort where I stayed overnight. Now, another

Here's the author about to take off in the Islander on that infamous "Seven Come Eleven" flight in 1988.

little airline was doing somewhat the same kind of schedule. Its assigned identifier was seven, and guess what its flight number was: seven-eleven (711)!

Do I need to go on?

I'm on final and cleared to land long, while somebody else, behind me, is cleared to land short on a runway that intersects the international's main runway, on which 711 is on final with a "heavy" on long final behind him. The controller asked *me* to perform a manoeuvre he intended for 711; not surprisingly he got his sevens and elevens mixed up. Though I was flummoxed by his request, I had to comply. This involved performing a manoeuvre that continues even now to disturb my

sleep. I was told to pull up and do a left turn back to the Iona jetty and to hold north of the jetty. I was about to land short of the intersection to the main runway—the pull-up and turn put me dangerously close to the airspace associated with the main runway, which the other plane and the heavy were using. The controller had intended it for the 711 aircraft because the heavy was getting too close behind him for comfort.

Luckily, it all worked out fine and nobody was put at risk. But give me Alpha Romeo Tango (ART), even if it is prefaced by a Foxtrot (F), over those numbers eleven-oh-seven vs. seven-eleven any day of the week.

6

OF MORTALITY

"No Man Is an Island" Sorts of Things

On Not Letting Go

In the movie *About Schmidt*, actor Jack Nicholson does a great job portraying the agonies of the middle manager of an insurance company who has just received the golden handshake. Nicholson's character is astounded when he meets his replacement: a falsely polite, callow youth with little experience. He is further dismayed when his pet project is trashed by the young man, and, before he can come to grips with the crushing effect of his retirement, his wife of 42 years drops dead. The movie brings some unpleasant realities into sharp relief: not simply the agonies of being pushed aside, but the ultimate reality that we are mortal.

John Donne summed up mortality back in about 1624, and no one has ever said it better: "No man is an island, entire of itself ... any man's death diminishes me, because I am involved in mankind; and therefore never send to know for whom the bell tolls; it tolls for thee."

How do you compete with that?

George, a pilot acquaintance of mine, has seven logbooks, beautifully maintained through the 46 years of his flying career. At age 19 he was flying the B.C. coast in a military Norseman floatplane, and at age 70 he was helping to rebuild a Norseman in the hangar of the British Columbia Aviation Museum. George's immaculate logbooks attest to his attitude about flying airplanes; but, more than that, they are a minute-by-minute record of his entire life, except for the time outs for meals and girl chasing. How does an aviator like that handle retirement? In George's case, he just stayed involved in some other aspect of the business. George wrote about his adventures for an aviation magazine, and he volunteered his services at the museum. In his mind he was still involved with aviation, even though he wasn't flying his old Norseman or a Goose or his favourite Citation jet.

Another pilot friend, always an avid amateur artist, now draws and paints and sells his beautiful aviation art. Art Cox helped to illustrate this book. He flew in the Royal Canadian Air Force, and then commercially for 25 years with Howard Hughes's famous airline, TWA. Art then served several years in the Middle East with Royal Jordanian Airlines. He too has a book in progress. Do chartered accountants do this sort of thing when they retire?

"Limited Palette," the first of the following stories, is fiction, but it deals with how one man couldn't let go of his pilot persona. John Donne's grasp of mortality is touched upon in the second story, "Missing from Life," and again in "Here's Mud in Your Eye." "Cold Case" is a poignant account of putting two and two together to solve an old puzzle, while "Stone Propellers" recalls the sadness when the end happens too soon. "Goodbye, 751" is fictionalized, but the experience is real, and I suspect that the pilot in this story went on to do what George or Art, or somebody else I can think of, did to keep the passion alive. This book ends with a letter to a friend that seems to sum it all up.

When John Travolta shows up wearing a captain's uniform for Qantas Airlines, most women cave in at the knees. All pilots see themselves as having some of that brand of charm, and throughout their careers—from Piper Cub to 747—they seem to do quite well in the romance department. So what happens when the suave and debonair captain retires and hangs up that chick-magnet uniform? Here's one possibility.

Limited Palette

I had four of those little brush pens: a red, a blue, a yellow, and, of course, a black. They are great for quick sketches, and a restaurant is a wonderful place to practise. I looked around the room to find a suitable subject and spotted a pretty young woman eating her lunch at a table that was two over from mine. She would be perfect, I thought, taking a sketch pad out of my briefcase. I don't like small sketch pads; I carry a nine by twelve and make no bones about what I'm doing. The restaurant was so busy with people coming and going and others waiting to be seated that no one took any notice of me—not even my waiter.

I started roughing in the scene with the young woman as the central focus. The sense of her aloneness with all the action going on around her is what I wanted the finished work to say. As I began to draw her, I realized she was gorgeous and dressed like a model. I loved examining her face to determine the exact line I would need to convey her sophistication. She had what I call a classic American nose, straight and fairly short. Her mouth was made up to look pouty. Her face was lean. I call this a class-one face, because it conforms to what *Vogue*, *Elle* and *Vanity Fair* magazines tell us is beauty. I couldn't disagree with them in this case. It was her eyes, though—wow! I'd never seen eyes like these, so that's what I exaggerated slightly in the drawing.

I think I captured the essence of her in as few strokes as possible. Her position in the chair was relaxed, but she couldn't help looking sexy, and I kind of overdid that by lengthening her legs a bit—which didn't hurt the drawing. She was wearing striped stockings, which she didn't mind displaying from the ankle on up past the knee, and a sort of slouchy hat that set off her beautiful face. Once I had the basic form of the subject and the "block-in" of the surrounding people, I would work in the colours to delineate and emphasize the action of the surrounding scene. But for now, the black brush was doing all the work. I blocked in the other figures: the waiters and busboys as well as guests seated, standing, eating, reading—all that stuff that could be treated in detail later. For now, I had

to capture this lonely beauty while she was here.

All this sketching involved much staring at her, then returning my attention to the drawing pad. During this process, I started falling in love with my subject, as I inevitably do when they are beautiful like this woman. I was busy examining her face when she looked up and our eyes met. She would be used to being looked at, so I wasn't surprised when she simply resumed eating her meal.

Changing brushes now, I started working with the blue for the blocked-in shadows surrounding her eyes and down the shadow side of her face. When I looked up again, she was staring at me. I didn't smile or in any way acknowledge that I was looking at her. I just turned back to my drawing pad, hoping she would go back to her meal. But she didn't, and when I looked again, she was still staring at me, but now with a resigned look on her gorgeous face. She stood up, but didn't remove her coat from the back of her chair, so unless she was heading for the girls' room, she was going to come over and give me what for, the way she probably told a lot of guys to get lost. I busied myself with my brushes, but could see out of the corner of my eye that she was making her way around the chairs and tables that separated us. She moved

just like she looked. This woman made her own music.

She put her hands on the chair back across from me and stared very coldly across the table. I filed that look away for future reference. It was a haughty look: high-arching eyebrows, level gaze with pupils dead centre in the eye and white showing under each iris. You have to note these things, or you would never be able to reproduce the effect on paper.

"Sir"—she put a lot of ice in that one word—"would you kindly mind your own business and stop staring at me, or I will dial nine-one-one. If you don't have anything better to do than … Oh! … Oh, that's wonderful … I didn't realize …"

She came around the table and stood beside me, to my right. She was tall, as I had determined previously from sketching her legs. I found myself looking up at her as she studied the drawing.

Somewhere along the way, the artist

stops observing and the man takes over. Truth is, the man has to be there first, or there wouldn't be the artist. I didn't come up with that, by the way; I think Picasso or somebody famous like him said it. I concluded that it was the man who was now observing his model with more than artistic interest as she picked up the sketch to examine it.

"This is very, very good. You must be a professional artist."

"Not really," I replied. "It's just a passion I've always had. You have to appreciate that it's not completed—just blocked in."

"Oh, it's wonderful. You certainly captured the noise and all the hubbub around here."

The two businessmen at the next table each looked up at different times to admire her, then returned to their Dow Jones Average. I put my pens away in their case and pocketed them. The artist was now definitely subordinated to the man, and I asked her if she would sit down and join me. She smiled, a seven-on-the-Richter-scale smile, but declined the invitation; her lunch remained unfinished on the other table. I took the bull by the horns and caught a passing waiter's attention. The young man wasn't happy about it, but he brought her lunch over and supplied her with fresh cutlery and serviettes, then went over and got her coat for her.

There was a real rose in a stem vase on the empty table beside us. I placed it in front of her in mock ceremony.

"Welcome to table 46. My name is Max." I offered my hand and she extended hers. I was reluctant to let go.

"I'm Jennelle," she said, withdrawing her hand.

Of course you are, I thought. Instead I replied, "*Enchanté.*"

"Oh, are you a French artist?" she asked with amusement.

"No, but I spend a lot of time in Paris. I like their expressions. Enchanté beats 'How are ya?' In any case, you must know Paris, in your business."

"In my business?" She looked a little suspicious of just exactly what I considered her business to be.

"I figured you as a fashion model."

"Oh, sure, a fashion model!" She broke into laughter. "Mister Max, I think you are hitting on me."

"Touché—of course I am," I said. "But I've drawn a lot of people, and you certainly have the face and figure."

That brought a knowing smile.

"Oh, I think you are a professional artist, all right. I think your art has worked for you." She dazzled me again with that smile. "A fashion model— really. Isn't that a bit of an obvious ploy? I work over on Howe Street, with the Employment Insurance office." She had a lovely laugh.

"Unemployment Insurance!" I didn't have to feign amazement. "What a waste. They sure didn't have the likes of you when I was on the dole."

"That must have been some time ago," she stated. "It's not called 'Unemployment' Insurance anymore; it's called 'Employment Insurance.' Been that way for some time now."

"Well, that dates me. I haven't drawn pogey since my training days."

"Training?"

"I'm an airline pilot," I explained. "Or was," I added with some reluctance.

"Oh, that explains everything," she laughed. "You thought I was a stewardess."

We both laughed at that. I insisted that I'd truly had her pegged as a model, and she explained that she was in fact an actuary with UI, or rather EI, as they now called it.

"Well, there you are," I said to that revelation. "You work with figures. As do I."

She gave me a sort of exasperated look, but not an unkind one, and I could see she was preparing to take her leave.

"I'm afraid I must go, but I really enjoyed meeting you ... " She paused before using my name. "... Captain Max. A lovely lunch hour—I will remember it." Another one of her dynamite smiles.

"Wait. Before you leave, please accept my drawing as a memento, and please look at this." I handed her the airline ticket envelope from my breast pocket and explained, "That's a ticket to Paris, departing next Wednesday. It's a pass, really. As an ex-pilot with that airline I can travel anywhere in the world on a pass, and ... " I paused.

She looked up.

"I'm allowed a guest."

She dabbed her lips with her serviette, giving me an incredulous look over the napkin, and was about to speak. I put up my hand to stay her.

"Don't say it. I know your reaction. Just keep Paris on your mind—Paris for a week, or two weeks, whatever. When you are working with those numbers at the EI, think of the Louvre, the Musée d'Orsay ... a dinner cruise down the Seine."

She was on her feet now, pulling on her coat, shaking her head with amused disbelief. It was a good sign. I pressed my point.

"I have an apartment in the Marais. Louis XIV, the Sun King, built it for his lady friends." In truth, it belonged to my friend Ed Paul, but what the hell ...

She was leaving now, smiling and giving me a goodbye wave.

"Jennelle." She stopped when I used her name and looked back, smiling indulgently.

"Read Hemingway's *A Moveable*

Feast. Let it become part of you. I wrote my phone number on the back of the drawing. Call me. The flight leaves next Wednesday. Bring only one bag—one that fits in the overhead compartment. And remember, no gels or sharp objects."

She grinned and waved as if to turn me off. I wanted to tell her that Hemingway wrote the memoir while living on Rue du Cardinal Lemoine in the Latin Quarter, not far from my apartment, but she was gone.

The busboy wanted to know if there was anything else. I didn't tell him that I had never been served. It was, after all, as much my fault as the waiter's, I'd been so engrossed in my drawing. He started to clear the table, and told me he had seen the drawing.

"Hey, that was a great drawing. You're really good." The young man handed me my glasses case. "She was a beautiful lady—your friend, I mean."

"Yes," I said. "Really lovely."

He was a nice young man, I thought, probably a university student. He was being quite attentive and was sort of grinning at me slyly.

"I'll bet being an artist helped you meet the ladies back in your day, sir?" It seemed he sort of added the "sir" so as not to be too cheeky. I didn't answer him, because I was cleaning my glasses on the tablecloth. When I looked up, he was still grinning at me.

"I mean, what woman could resist having her picture painted? Man, I could meet a lot of chicks with a talent like yours!"

He reached under the table directly beneath my feet. "Don't forget your cane, sir, and watch that step down at the door."

When I looked back from the door, he called to me.

"Maybe you could give me lessons, sir. You could teach me everything you know, maybe even drawing lessons."

I ignored the young man's remarks while damn near tripping on that unexpected step at the door. I wondered if I would ever get used to those bloody bifocals.

Most of us don't fork much lightning during our lives. When we check out, our legacy fades pretty fast. The Jerome Kern/Oscar Hammerstein classic "Ol' Man River" might be referring to planting cotton, but the sentiment is universal: "Them that plants 'em is soon forgotten." For the short period that we remain in living memory, we might be surprised about what we are remembered for. The coastal pilot of this story left several legacies: the one described here is his best. Unfortunately, only a few would appreciate his bequest.

Missing from Life

When people leave life unexpectedly, an energy remains long after they are gone. I'm thinking of Ed, a pilot I knew, who had been working on a major plan to expand his little floatplane airline when he suddenly disappeared on a flight one foggy morning. He was never found.

Ed had been working on a chain of docks at Alert Bay that would allow him to serve that popular village destination on any tide. At low tide, two of the floats extended into water deep enough for a floatplane; at high tide, the aircraft could be conveniently loaded right at the main road, adjacent to the business section of town. When it was my plane that used these docks rather than his, I found that he had not completed the job. The sea anchor that had been planned to hold the docks in place had not been installed, but the concrete blocks and chains to do the

job were on the beach where he had
assembled them. Another pilot and I
were able to haul these out to the end
of the docks and place them in the exact position he had planned: the chains
were the right length, and everything
worked as our missing benefactor had
planned. Those docks remained in
place for several years.

Down in Kelsey Bay, there was
other evidence of Ed's vitality and
sound business sense. He had built a
passenger waiting room in the bush
beside the seaplane dock, next to the
home of his dispatcher on the Salmon
River. It was almost completed, requiring only a connection to hydro
to power the lights and the electric
baseboard heater he had installed. His
business plan was evident here too.
Anyone requiring a flight into one
of the numerous logging camps and
Native villages of the B.C. mid-coast
could now safely leave a vehicle here
at Kelsey Bay and fly into camp. This
convenience beat driving an additional
100-odd miles to Port McNeill or Port
Hardy to catch a plane. To cover all
the bases, Ed had bought an abandoned boathouse on the shore of Port
McNeill's harbour, some 60 air miles up
the coast. This building had a marine
railway extending out to the low tide
line. Ed had planned to winch his aircraft ashore for maintenance and repair.

For many years after Ed disappeared, these elements of his projects
remained in place and were used by
me as well as by others. They were
constant reminders of the man's pres-
ence, of his sheer energy during his
lifetime—cut short as it was.

One day I landed at Alert Bay
and found his docks were gone.
The municipality had installed a
government-owned seaplane dock. A
little later, the Port McNeill facility
fell to the demands of other harbour
developments. Now Ed remained only
a memory in the minds of those who
once knew him, some of whom were
no longer an active part of the local
scene. That missing pilot's foresight and
business acumen had followed him into
obscurity.

Not long ago, I flew past Kelsey
Bay and thought again about Ed. I
wondered if his waiting room—black
Naugahyde chrome-armed chairs, electric coffee maker and all—had given
up waiting and had now been totally
reclaimed by the forest.

The DH82C
Tiger Moth was
built in quantity
for elementary
flying training
with the British
Commonwealth
Air Training Plan
during the Second
World War. Trainees
would graduate from
the Moth onto the
Harvard, for fighter
pilot types, or onto
the twin-engined
Avro Anson, for those
selected as bomber
pilots.

JACK SCHOFIELD
1946

People who choose to live in the backwoods are not much different from city folk. However, certain relationships that might draw critical comment in the big city go unnoticed in the wilderness. Whether this is due to the fact that few people live in the wilds, or that those who do are more understanding, is a moot point.

Here's Mud in Your Eye

In a place called Lagoon Cove, deep within the beautiful waterways of the B.C. mid-coast rainforest, lived a young, recently wed couple who operated a small sport-fishing resort.

Well, there are two corrections to that opening statement. She was young, about 20, and he was about 45, a quarter century her senior; and, as this story happened a long time ago, the "recently wed" statement is now inaccurate. Perhaps "once upon a time" would be more apt.

He was a friendly guy, very industrious, with an infectious sense of humour. When we had freight or passengers, he would help me load the plane and would tell me how he had taken flying lessons on a Tiger Moth. I too had learned to fly on a Tiger Moth, so we had some basis for conversation. We had each performed aerobatics and shared the experience of being blinded by dirt falling into our eyes from the cockpit floor when flying upside down, and we agreed that flying an open-cockpit biplane was a very special experience. We had pretty well exhausted the topic after my third or fourth flight into the resort that first summer.

I recall now that Frank (I never knew his last name) never got past the simple statement that he had taken flying lessons, and I gathered more from what he didn't say than what he did: he never finished those lessons. For fear of invading his privacy, I never pressed the point; and he always became very quiet when he had the opportunity to explain. Much later, I would appreciate why he quit talking, but for that first and second summer when I flew his guests into the cove, it remained an unimportant question mark.

I did learn a few things, though, about Frank and his child bride during those two seasons. I overheard them talking with obvious concern one day. He said something like "You'll be left with nothing," to which she replied, "I'll have the memory of our love," and then they embraced while I quickly skidded out of view and made my way back to the plane.

The next season rolled around, and as the summer progressed I mentioned to my dispatcher that we hadn't received a call from Lagoon Cove. He was startled and said, "Oh, didn't you hear? That guy, the older guy married to that young girl—he dropped dead on the dock last Christmas. People say he had a congenital heart disorder. The lodge is shut down. Don't know where she got to."

I was shocked. "Well, that's really too bad," I remember saying. "He and I were … well. We both learned to fly on a Tiger Moth."

"Really? He flew?"

"Yeah. In an open-cockpit biplane. Loved the experience."

I wondered where the young woman had gone. I would have liked to tell her about how he got dirt in his eyes from flying upside down; I think she would have liked to hear that.

There is a TV show that deals with solving old mysteries. Using modern-day forensic methods and DNA analysis, the TV cops bring aging criminals to account for their hitherto unsolved crimes. It's a great concept, because it is based on fact—as is this account of how the cause of a long-forgotten tragedy suddenly revealed itself.

Cold Case

Many years ago, a well-known pilot went missing on a charter flight. He was flying a Cessna 180 floatplane and was returning, alone, up Johnstone Strait. A search along his flight route located the missing plane floating upside down in turbulent waters. There was no sign of the pilot, and the aircraft was not structurally damaged. It was thought that it had landed on the water and overturned later, after the landing. There was much speculation, but little in the way of hard facts. Nor was there a CSI type of investigation of accidents in those days, and the tragedy remained a mystery forever.

Well, not quite. Twenty-odd years later, Al Beaulieu, who had salvaged the Cessna from the waters, needed some parts for a Cessna 180's engine and, while rummaging through his salvaged aircraft parts, came across the complete engine

Search and rescue aircraft of 442 Squadron, from CFB Comox, holding for weather at Port Hardy during a search in 1981 for Cessna C-FZSZ. This Cessna went missing on a flight from Kingcome to the head of Knight Inlet.

134

and other remains of that ill-fated Cessna. Al removed the parts he needed and took them to his workbench to disassemble and inspect them. The part he was looking for was an internally mounted shaft that operated inside the engine's fuel pump. When he opened up the salvaged fuel pump, there, before his eyes, was the cause of the accident. That little shaft was in two pieces. It had obviously failed, and the Cessna's engine had quit from fuel starvation. The pilot had made good the deadstick landing, but the water on which he had landed is notoriously rough from the high winds that gust from a nearby river mouth. The aircraft likely overturned during the landing or while drifting in those whitecapping waters. The pilot might have clung to the floats for a while, but eventually he would have been swept away or killed by exposure.

When Al opened the fuel pump, he gasped with the poignant realization that the old mystery had been solved. Although this revelation obviously was of no help to the long-deceased pilot, a measure of closure had been achieved.

Flying is a lot safer than driving home from the airport, but accidents do happen, and for a variety of reasons: weather and pilot error seem to figure large in these tragedies. Here are the stories of two pilots who never had the chance for a lifetime achievement award, because their lives ended too soon to qualify.

Stone Propellers

Al Beach

Al Beach is the kid on the extreme left in the picture on the following page. He has sort of a smirk on his face and probably has just said something funny. Only two days after this photo was taken, he became a headline in both Vancouver newspapers, having flown into the rocks of Cape Roger Curtis on Bowen Island in a B.C. Airlines Seabee flying boat. Al was a very good student pilot, and the first of ten of us to get work flying an airplane. Bill Sylvester, the famous founder of B.C. Airlines, signed Al up, had him checked out in the Seabee and turned him loose. He did a couple of hundred hours on the coast and was reported to be a hit with some nurses up at the Alert Bay hospital.

One foggy morning Al took off from Vancouver airport carrying two passengers.

Pilots in training in 1946 pose with a B.C. Aero Club Tiger Moth. During the post-war years this Vancouver-based flying club boasted a membership of 600, many of whom were non-flying "social members." Left to right: Al Beach; unknown; "Jet" Popel; unknown; the author; Edith, the club secretary; Ken Kirk; Nick Percival; two unknown. On top: Chuck Wilson. "Jet" Popel later drove a city bus in Vancouver. Ken Kirk flew 747s for CP Air. Nick Percival won B.C. Amateur Pilot and became captain of DC-8s with British West Indies Air; he married a flight attendant, then died suddenly from Lou Gehrig's disease. Chuck Wilson went on to win the Webster Trophy and become safety pilot for CP Air.

STAN BUDD PHOTO

136

His first checkpoint along the way was to be Bowen Island, but he found the morning fog too dense for comfort, so he let down carefully through the crud and touched down on the water perfectly—planning, apparently, to wait until the fog burned off. Unfortunately, he was dead on course—excuse the play on words—and immediately after touching down, he struck the rocks of fog-shrouded Bowen Island. His two passengers survived, but Al didn't make it.

Less than a week after this photo was taken, the young guys draped around and over this old Tiger Moth biplane attended a funeral and heard Al's fiancée cry out from behind the curtained family area of the funeral parlour. Then they watched as their friend was interred beneath a stone propeller bearing his name and two dates that were only 19 years apart.

Bob d'Easum

Bob d'Easum was early into the fray. He was the second of our group of newly arrived 100-hour wonders to be hired as a pilot. Pacific Western Airlines had just bought out everybody on the coast and had established a base at Ocean Falls, where Bob resided with a new model of Cessna aircraft known as the 180. It would become famous,

The seaplane ramp at Ocean Falls, where Bob d'Easum was based, was built for the Mallard flying boats that served this paper mill town for 26 years. Now Ocean Falls is a ghost town, and many of its buildings have been sold and moved out on barges. The concrete ramp, however, remains as a reminder of the town's glory days.

but Bob wouldn't. Bob complained to head office maintenance about this 180; it had something wrong with it. What was it that was wrong, engineering asked, and Bob could say only that his ass told him something was wrong: it wasn't turning up the right take-off rpm, and it didn't sound right. Sounding right is not an engineering priority, and Bob's ass wasn't listed as a maintenance guideline. He was told to fly the Cessna until his tour of duty was over, then bring it down to Vancouver. They would take a look at it then.

Well, he didn't bring it back to them, and they were left with all those technical logbooks with no airplane to match. What do you do with tech logs and no airplane? The accident investigation guys had an answer for that: they would go over the logs to see if something obvious had caused the 180 to disappear.

The accident investigator had a couple of coffees and a cigarette while scanning the book, but found nothing significant. The logbook was thrown into a file box in the corner of the office. Nor did the search planes that scoured the waterways near Ocean Falls and all the way up to Kitimat find anything significant. Despite the efforts of Bob's mother, newspaper columnist Lille d'Easum, who exercised her influence to keep the search going, the search and rescue squadron stopped searching, and there was no rescue. Bob joined the legion of lost aviators on B.C.'s wild coast.

On a very hot day in June 1981, 20 years later, a massive air search was conducted to find a lost Beaver aircraft that had taken off from Klemtu with Ocean Falls as its destination. Among the seven passengers aboard was a friend of Pierre Trudeau, then the prime minister. The short distance between Klemtu and Ocean Falls narrowed the search area significantly, but weeks went by with no sign of the AirBC Beaver. The Comox-based search master was instructed to keep searching until the plane was found.

The RCMP brought in a newly developed underwater search device known as a side-scanning sonar. Employing the device, the marine detachment locked onto something that looked very much like an aircraft resting in deep water along the likely route of the missing Beaver. Tests on oil samples that had come to the surface in the area confirmed that it was likely aircraft oil. A barge with a crane was brought in, and after much difficulty it was hooked onto the object and began a careful lifting operation. The object had been hoisted halfway to the surface when news broke that the Beaver had been found hanging in the trees just short of Ocean Falls. All its crew and passengers were dead. The barge dropped the object and went home.

This story proves that a prime minister has a lot more clout than a mere newspaper columnist, but if Lille d'Easum had been alive, she would have raised enough hell that the "object" on the end of the crane's line would have been brought to the surface. Chances are that the fate of her son, Bob, would have been confirmed, and the authorities would have had a plane to fit those logbooks. I suppose this would have brought some satisfaction to Mrs. d'Easum; but as it happened, she had attained closure in the more usual way.

The press loved it and ran it on the front page under a bold 18-point column header. The text continued on page A7, where many photos and vox pop letters supported the article. "A SHIP IS NOT A SHE," the headline yelled, and the text rang with Gloria Steinem–type indignation. Our social awareness at this time was at the intersection of Women's Lib and Political Correctness, and spokespersons for abolishing the gender of inanimate objects like ships and airplanes were rampant. They also wanted an order-in-council banning the gender designation of pipe fittings to describe how one fit into the other. The House of Commons demurred, but support for the change was offered by many industries that could not afford to offend.

Goodbye, 751

He heard the familiar bark of the main gear as the rubber kissed the runway. The incisions that had recently been cut across the touchdown area of the asphalt on runway 27 eliminated any fear of hydroplaning, despite the heavy downpour that was now reflecting in the twin beams of the 737's landing lights. His "second dickey" was reaching out to perform the reverse thrust, but he decided to do it himself and knocked Ray Goodman's hand away. Ray smiled, knowingly, and made some facial expressions that were facetiously meant to say, "Hey, man, she's your ship." At least for this one last time—that would be what Ray was thinking, he mused. He had felt the man's covetous glances toward the pilot seat for the last few days and had developed an unfamiliarly brittle attitude toward his co-pilot, who he calculated would gladly slip into the left seat while the leather was still warm. Nuts to you, he thought. Wait your turn. She's mine until the last blade in the turbines rattles to a stop.

She slowed to taxi speed right where he'd planned it, at the Whiskey intersection, where the little blue runway lights shone through the downpour, pointing out the path to the terminal. Ray had got the message and was completely hands off. He was making entries in the journey log, leaving the airplane to the pilot. Good, he thought. Every man to his trade. He was still PIC—pilot in command—even if for the last time.

He thought that 36 years on the flight deck should be running through his mind like an in-flight movie, but it wasn't happening that way. He was simply doing what he had always done, minding the ship, and she was doing just as he bid. No flashback recollections of DC-6Bs thundering down the runway en route to Tokyo, with a fuel stop in the Aleutians; no Connies with their flame-throwing exhausts; his favourite, the Lockheed L-1011, didn't show up; and his stint of flying sideways in 747s was now such ancient history that those days and his then shiny, unlined brow were relegated to his mental ashcan.

One thing did come to mind, though: the camaraderie of the early days. Friendly, tight-knit crews had made it all a real adventure. And who'd ever heard of a flight attendant in those days? They were "stews," and they were as much part of the crew as the pilots, navigators and flight engineers. All the newfangled cockpit crew integration programs couldn't replace the team spirit they had back then. And the aircraft: significantly, this '37 was the first one he had flown and, like him, it was destined for the scrap heap sooner rather than later. His hands gripped the power levers, and he censured himself for getting maudlin.

There was a guy in a yellow slicker doing tai chi with two lighted batons, signalling him into the passenger bay. Did that guy really think he had any part in parking this airplane? The pilot put the nose wheel on the yellow line, followed it around to the tennis ball and spooled down. "Slazenger" was printed on the yellow ball, which was now against the windshield.

The big rubber bellows on the end of the gangplank came out, slowly, to engulf the now open passenger door. He always thought of it as a giant vacuum inhaling the passengers from the plane.

He performed the shutdown check by rote, then sat there for a minute looking at the panel. The fact that it was the last time he would do this began to sink in, and he wondered why it had to be. At 60 he was as fit as ever and held a category-one medical, completed only two weeks ago. Ray was watching him with a half smile on his face, and the stew—whoops, the flight attendant, Julie, who was also the shop steward for the "stews," the flight attendants' union—came on the intercom and asked him to open the door (the $10,000 security door) because she needed to speak to him. We didn't have bulletproof doors, either, he thought as Ray threw the latch.

Julie was smiling, and behind her all the passengers were standing at their seats, smiling and clapping.

She addressed him: "Captain, these passengers and the hundreds and hundreds of other passengers you have flown over the past 35 years applaud your skill and years of service. We all extend our hope that your retirement years will be happy and fulfilling."

A lot of cheering and clapping followed. Somebody called out, "What's your favourite airplane?"

The captain stood up, embarrassed but pleased by the gesture, and replied, "This very airplane is the first 737 I ever flew, and she's my favourite."

"Why would this one be any different from the others?" This question from the same guy. "If they changed the paint job, how would you tell one from the other?"

"If your wife wore a new dress, would you recognize her?" Everybody laughed at his response.

Then Julie came back on. "Ladies and gentlemen, our company has adopted the policy that discourages the use of the feminine gender for our airplanes, but our retiring captain is excused. Old habits die hard. This aircraft has the manufacturer's tail number of 751, and that's how we now refer to her ... ah, I mean to it." She blushed a little and laughed, as did the passengers as they filed out the door. Some of the men reached out and shook his hand as they departed, and a blowsy woman threw her arms around him, laughingly exclaiming that she just loved pilots.

Later, he walked across the tarmac, past the maintenance hangar and toward the crew parking lot. There she was, standing, or rather crouching, before the hangar door. Her navigation lights blinked back at him from the reflecting pools of rainwater on the asphalt as he passed. He noted the movement inside the well-lit cabin— cleaners at work—and the honey wagon alongside, doing its odious job. A van marked "Commissary" hissed past him on its way to replenish the galley as he punched the combination for the gate and entered the parking lot.

He thought of Millie, gone now for two years and apparently happy with a

The end of a summer flying day could mean the pilot had been flying for 12 hours. He would have been up for 13 hours, grabbing meals at logging camps while on the run. There are rules about this, but in the bush, who's looking?

nine-to-five guy in New West. He regretted that she wouldn't be there when he got home tonight. She had always been cheerful and would have had a stiff gin and tonic waiting for him, on this of all nights. "What the hell," she would have said, "it's only a job."

His headlights shone through the chain-link fence and reflected off 751. He saw her crouching in the rain as he turned out of the lot onto Grant McConachie Way.

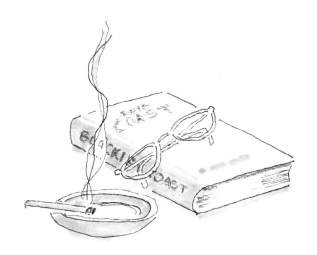

The coastal seaplane airlines were the training ground for many young pilots as they worked their way up to fly the "heavy iron" of the major carriers. Not this guy—he hung in for 40 years, flying floatplanes for most of the gypo operators on the coast. When one employer insisted that he wear a tie, he cut the neckpiece in half and gave the knotted end to his boss. Then he left to set up his own little operation out of Sechelt, B.C. It's not that he did anything really special, just that he sort of personifies the industry and the way it was—and, let me tell you, this man could tell stories. Unfortunately, those two packs a day took him off the flight line before we could record the many anecdotes he had collected during his colourful life.

A Letter to Blackie

Dear Blackie,

I have one of those big plastic wall-mounted monthly planning charts, and on it is your name, underlined on the square labelled January 22. It was there to remind me of the date we'd set for our first session of writing your book—the book to be titled *Blackie's Coast*.

Blackie, you're not going to make that appointment, and I'm having trouble—I don't want to erase your name. You see, whether you knew it or not, you personified the so-called romance of flight—you and that video produced by the Knowledge Network as a "B.C. Moment." All those great scenes of you flying your Beaver along the coast, the split-S turns over Chatterbox Falls and the idyllic scene from inside the cockpit with your physiog in profile and our beautiful shoreline going by like it

144

Jack Apsouris (Blackie) with "Blossom" on the dock of the Bayshore Inn at Vancouver Harbour, about 1989. Jack's daughter Lindsey has his logbooks, which tell of a private licence in 1955 and flying his first Beaver in 1957.

PHOTOGRAPHER UNKNOWN

does for everyone who flies a seaplane up and down this coast.

You were a one-man show, Blackie—the way we would all like to operate, and the way it was, in the beginning, for most of us. We all envied you, and while there were those who probably cursed you for your rugged individualism and ingrained ways, you had it all and could laugh at us from your noisy perch in the sky.

While most of us flew for commercial endeavours, you always seemed to be doing the fun things, like flying for the CBC TV shows *The Beachcombers* and *Danger Bay*. Hell, you even looked more like Nick Adonidas than Bruno Gerussi did. And naming your Beaver "Blossom," such an appropriate name for an ugly plug like a DHC-2—why didn't I think of that?

The only thing that burns me about you, Blackie, is how you stole the show when Peter Gzowski on CBC Radio's *Morningside* interviewed you and me and Al Beaulieu. Al and I stuttered some inane replies to Gzowski's questions, while you sailed in with one of your inimitable tall stories and left us looking like dumbbells.

Blackie, all those great stories you were going to have me write have gone with you now and won't be in a book for others to enjoy. Your name on my calendar will ultimately get rubbed out to make way for another appointment, but I promise you this: your name won't be rubbed off my memory. I'm going to carry it there until you and I join up for some tight formation work in other skies. Until then, thanks for being another coastal pilot and a good friend.

Jack (Blackie) Apsouris
1934–Christmas Eve 1996